THE
THEOLOGIANS
OF ORION

Ronnie Theroux

The Theologians of Orion

ISBN 979-8-9859022-0-4

This book is dedicated to the two humans
who have my whole heart.

Based on a True Story

Contents

PREFACE

Throughout her life she wanted to know the unknown. She desperately wanted to know how life got to this planet and to know if God really exists. Never in her life would she imagine that she would get what she asked for and discover who she was.

CHAPTER 1

The Awakening

It started from the time she was very young, but it would take her decades to come to her awakening to who she is. Her awakening process began in 2012, the year the Mayan calendar ended and the year hundreds of thousands of others were also waking up. Among those was her mother. This story sheds light on life outside this world, about God, and a big secret that no one on Earth knows. Her name is Sydney, and this is her story.

It was 2012 and after several month-long battles with an illness from mold, she had to leave her position at the company she had been with for many years. It was a great job as she was making the most money she had ever made. She had worked hard and smart to be considered one of the top managers in the male-dominated field of construction. At the time, she remembered a strong feeling that she needed to sell her home and belongings because this sickness was going to be a long haul, but something else was there. There was another reason this was happening, but she couldn't put her finger on it. She brushed this feeling off as she had always done.

Sydney sold her home, put her belongings in storage, and moved in with a friend. During this time away, she started to feel better and after so many years of stress encompassing her entire life, she finally had time to reflect on the things she constantly thought of in prior years and growing up. For some reason, she was always fascinated with the Church, God, and thoughts on how life got to this planet.

Sydney had a lot of time on her hands, so she started researching the origins of life. She had been so deeply involved in her work that she stopped watching television and paying attention to the world around her. She was stepping into another world. Unbeknownst to her, her mother was also going through an awakening, drawing pictures of strange beings and people.

Sydney couldn't shake this new feeling that came into her mind when doing this research. It began to consume her mind. While searching the internet, she came across an upcoming UFO conference. She had heard of these conferences before, but the idea of going to one wasn't all that appealing. She felt that she would be amongst a lot of techie people and people who dressed strangely. She had a very strong feeling that she needed to go to this conference anyway. It was February of 2013 when Sydney was making her way to a UFO conference in Arizona by herself.

She landed at the airport and took a thirty-minute ride to the hotel where the conference was being held and where she would be staying for two nights. Sydney unpacked her things and then went downstairs to check out the conference rooms. There was only a UFO movie going on, so she picked a seat to sit down and watch. Little did she know, she was sitting near the previous Director of the UFO conference, Donald Ware. He struck up a conversation with her and was nice and friendly. He must have sensed she was new to this as he took her under his wing and showed her around without even asking if she had been to a conference like this before. She was like a lost puppy following the nice man who would later invite her to lunch and dinners and introduce her to all his friends and some speakers. She finished the movie, said goodnight, then grabbed a bite to eat in the café and headed back to her room for an early night turn-in.

On the first day of the conference, she got herself showered and dressed for the day and then headed to the ground floor to the conference rooms. As soon as she stepped out of the elevator, she felt some kind of energy around her, around her shoulders. It felt really good, like a warm blanket wrapped around her. She thought to herself, "There's that feeling again, I haven't had this in a long time." She continued around the hotel with this feeling trying to shrug it off as if it was nothing, when the hotel doorman walked right up to her with wide eyes, shook her hand, and pointed above her shoulder. "There is something around you. I can see something with you," he said. Sydney then turned her head as the woman behind the counter said, "I see it too." "I can feel it, I don't know what it is," Sydney replied to them both. Now that two people saw this sparkling light of energy around her, she could not shrug this off as her imagination as she had done in the years prior.

Still surprised by this, she finished her business at the front desk, then made her way to the speakers' rooms. This would be a huge eye-opener because she had read about these reptilian beings weeks before and didn't know what to think of that. Barbara Lamb educated the audience on the reptilian beings and hybrids as Sydney sat there dumbfounded that this kind of talk was coming out of a sweet older woman who seemed perfectly normal.

The next day came, and the first speaker up was Dolores Cannon who was also going on about people she had regressed and their abduction stories. She went on about the volunteers here on Earth and Sydney identified with how she described lightworkers. She realized from the description that she had to be one as she felt different all of her life, but still didn't quite know what this meant. Sydney found the messages that came from these regressions to be amazing. These two women were her favorite speakers.

During a break from the speakers, Sydney went to visit the merchant area to buy an alien souvenir so she could remember her first UFO conference. As she looked around, she came to an end table she had to walk by to get to the other side. Sydney looked at what the lady was selling, and the woman said to her, "You are a lightworker." "Yes, I think so," Sydney replied. The woman then paused as if she was thinking and said, "They are telling me you are reconnecting with who you are." Sydney just looked at her and didn't know what to say. She was awestruck. After a brief pause, Sydney asked, "Who am I?" The woman looked at her almost like Sydney should know, but she didn't respond. Her words struck Sydney because something was happening, but she couldn't understand what. She experienced a sudden rush of old feelings, and said to herself, "What is going on here?" Sydney bought a video from the woman and then continued down the row to see what other interesting things were for sale. She couldn't stop thinking about the strange things that were going on and what she had just been told.

Sydney went to have lunch and while in line, asked the lady in front of her if she would like to share a table. The woman was nice and said yes. During their conversation, she learned that this lady and been taken many times. She believed her daughter was an alien hybrid and she had experienced being on a spaceship.

It then dawned on Sydney that most of the people at this conference were what you would call experiencers.

During her short time at the conference, Sydney met a few people and made a few friends. One of these friends asked why she was there, and she told him it was because her mother had seen a UFO many years ago. He said, "I think you should ask your mother for more details about that UFO sighting because there is something very different about you." Which she agreed to do when she got home.

Sydney made her rounds again at the merchant area where Mr. Ware was. She went to tell him goodbye, but he was occupied with a spiritual man who was selling something. The man said he wanted to hug Sydney and she accepted. The hug seemed a little awkward and a little too long. Mr. Ware butted in saying, "Let me do it, you're doing it wrong." He pushed the man aside and said something about aligning the chakras while giving this hug. And then the strangest thing happened. When Mr. Ware pulled away from the hug, she felt strong intense energy that started from her feet and ran up her body. She didn't even say anything about it because she was in shock. She walked away saying she had to go, asking herself over and over, "What is happening?"

Sydney went back to her hotel room and packed her things, called for her ride, and went to the airport. She talked to the cab driver about the conference and told him it was very strange but felt that most of what she learned from it was true. Once she was sitting at the airport, she spoke to a nice woman next to her about the experience as well. Sydney explained what she had seen and learned from the conference and all the strange things that happened. At that moment Sydney felt she had a mission; "I am supposed to give….. love?" This thought was just coming to her. The lady was very nice but did say it sounded crazy. Sydney didn't blame her.

Once Sydney was back home, the strange experiences continued. A couple of days later, Sydney was reading a Dolores Cannon book on the couch when she put the book down, looked to the ceiling, and said out loud, "Is this real? Is this stuff real?" She had a thought deep down that it was but, in her mind, she was just trying to process all the crazy stuff she was experiencing. She got up and moved to turn on a light in the dining room and two of the chandelier lights exploded, *"pop pop"*. Sydney jumped from the loud and sudden noise. She then went to turn the hall light on which too exploded with sparks flying. It felt as though this was a sign to her question and she got her answer. This stuff was real, and she was experiencing something very strange.

She wandered upstairs to go to bed and was trying to take in all this craziness and figured she was having some kind of awakening. She just didn't understand what was happening. The next morning, she was lying in bed between the state of sleep and awake when a picture came into her mind. It was a man in a white robe with a beard and long dark hair, standing on the edge of a path, turned slightly sideways to point in her direction. She looked at the man from his feet to his head and noticed he looked like an image of Jesus, but she didn't want to jump to the conclusion that he was. In her mind, Sydney asked, "Why am I seeing this?" At that moment Sydney was shocked by the overwhelming feeling of unconditional love, enveloping her whole body. It was the most amazing feeling she ever felt. She laid there reveling in this feeling for as long as she could, as long as the feeling would last. It was then she understood who she was seeing.

It was so beautiful, so overwhelmingly beautiful. It was a love that she always wanted, one that she never found on Earth. She wanted to go with Jesus. She knew this was real. Later she wondered why she received the vision, and what it meant. She could only assume she received the vision as an answer to her question the night before, "Is this stuff real?" During the vision, she got the distinct message that Jesus was saying, "When you are ready, come walk the path with me, beside me." But why her and what did this mean?

A few days later, Sydney decided to have a past life regression to see if it would bring to light the information she might have been missing to understand the experiences she was going through. She was hopeful she could be put into the relaxed state that she needed to be in because she wasn't sure she could. The practitioner was Larry, and they did the regression over the computer. She told Larry about her mother's UFO sighting in the late fifties. He wanted to explore that and when she focused on her mother, she saw her on a table with a light on her face. Larry asked her to look around the room. Sydney saw a door that had a light coming into it, a very bright light. He said, "Focus on that; do you see anyone come through the door?" "Yes, a very tall man," Sydney answered. Larry began to take her to a previous life, back to her origins. The picture of Jesus holding out his hand extended appeared to her. She felt she was his child, that he was holding her in his cupped hand. "What year was this?" Larry asked. "Sixty-one," Sydney replied. The picture changed; she saw Jesus sitting on the ground, looking up at her with loving and adoring eyes. Larry then took her to another time, to the future, and she saw herself very happy and walking somewhere. She was walking on a sidewalk, near a courtyard with a water fountain. She was about to do something important. She got the feeling she was going to speak on an important issue even though normally she experiences stage fright. The regression ended there, and Sydney was unsure of what to think. It was her first regression, and she wasn't sure it worked as it was supposed to, or why those scenes appeared in her head.

The strange things continued when two days later, Sydney half awoke to a loud buzzing in her ear and a dream of a colorful bird that poked her in her right side with its beak. She swatted it and as it had been made of wood, it shattered. She got up and looked around and there was nothing in her room that could have made the loud buzzing noise. It was one of those dreams that weren't a dream if you can understand that. She realized she had pain in her side, where the bird in her dream had pecked her, which turned out to be caused by dehydration. Things were starting to come to her in a relaxed state that seemed like messages, and it felt strange.

Remembering to follow up with her friend who asked her to find out more about her mother's sighting, Sydney called her mother and asked about her UFO sighting. Her mother, Beverly explained that it happened in 1958 when she and her cousin were driving home from a drive-in movie. They were supposed to go straight home after the movie was over because her aunt would always sit up waiting for them. She had strict rules and told them not to stop off anywhere. In typical teenager fashion, they stopped off at a malt shop, then tried their best to hurry and get home before getting in big trouble. They were driving in Beverly's cousin's 1949 Plymouth Sedan when an object flew over them from behind, remained suspended in the air in front of them, and had somehow completely stopped their car. The radio went haywire with static. They both looked at each other in shock, then Beverly noticed her cousin had the *pedal to the metal, but they were going nowhere*. Beverly explained to Sydney she heard a sound like a rope swirling and the spaceship had a belt of crystals all around it. The crystal belt was spinning left while the remainder of the craft spun in the opposite direction. The crystals shined like lights in the moonlight and she noticed there were beings inside the craft.

The next thing they remembered was getting out of the car at home, five miles away, only Beverly was somehow in the driver's seat instead of her cousin. They walked up the stairs to the house while her cousin repeatedly said to Beverly, "I don't want to talk about it, I don't want to talk about it." Once inside, they found the aunt in bed which would have never happened. They both looked out the window and saw the spaceship which then suddenly zipped away. It was like it waited to be sure the girls got into the house safely before leaving.

By this time, after attending the UFO conference and reading up on the internet, Sydney recognized that her mother's description of what happened was what UFO researchers refer to as "missing time". During her conversation with her mom, Sydney told her, "Mom, you had missing time. That means you were taken." "Well, I must have been," her mother replied. Sydney was in shock thinking that these kinds of things happen to other people, not to her own family.

Sydney tried to end the call to process what she learned, when her mother said, "And you know, I don't know why, but I always think about God, the Bible, and how the Earth was populated." Sydney was confused because those were the thoughts she had all her life and she recognized right off that those were not her mother's thoughts. Someone was talking to her; she was channeling someone. She sat there and thought to herself, "This is so strange, what is going on with us and why now?"

Sydney's mother seemed to morph into a different person repeating sentences that were not something she would normally say.

"You do not see with your eyes and you do not hear with your ears.
You make your own heaven and hell on Earth.
Adam and Eve did not populate the Earth.
You no longer use your brains.

The people of Earth were given free will.

We are unhappy that you are destroying yourselves.

The grey beings are almost like you; they think in a straight line. They are programmed prototypes. We call the greys by the job they do; we call them Seekers and Retrievers.

When your DNA gets low, we pick you up and put an implant in your body so that we can upgrade your DNA."

"What in the hell is going on here? What is this?" Sydney demanded. Sydney knew her mom wouldn't make these things up. She started to ask questions about who this was and why they were contacting them, but no one seemed to reply. Sydney got off the phone with her mother in complete shock and confusion.

Here she attended a UFO conference and suddenly, both she and her mother were having crazy experiences and strange communication, but this was just the beginning. There was so much more in store for Sydney. She was about to receive the shock of her life.

CHAPTER 2

Initial Contact

Sydney continued receiving visions and had a lot of dream interactions. In one dream she was outdoors camping which she hadn't done in about twenty years and at this point never thought she would again. She saw herself outdoors with friends watching a group of UFOs in the sky. Then she saw herself lying down with a blanket at a campsite. She saw a grey alien which scared her and told it to go away. As she lay in her bed, she was shaking her head back and forth saying, "No". Just then everything went black, and she heard a screeching sound in her head, like a cassette tape being rewound. A few weeks later she would be invited to go camping with friends and saw the same scene that she saw in her dream, excluding the grey alien. She couldn't believe this had come true. A few days later she called a person who investigates sightings, who said other people had reported the same thing about the cassette sound in their head.

Three weeks later in another dream, very colorful flowers were popping up from the ground. Then a shirtless man with a potbelly arrived from the skies above and landed on the grass. Three beautiful girls landed from the sky around him, and he asked Sydney if she wanted to go. She understood he was there to remove her from her daily pain and take her back home. Through her mind, she told the man she wasn't ready, that she still had work to do.

A few days later Sydney received a vision that drifted across her eyes that she also felt. This happened during the day when she was at her mother's house and while she was awake. It went from her right eye to the left and it was a picture of a long white wall with a shorter block wall that had an arched opening. She asked her mother what it was and was told to figure it out. But she knew it was Jesus' tomb even before searching for the picture on the internet. She felt strongly that she was given these experiences so that she could understand what her mother was also experiencing. But a vision of Jesus' tomb, now that was astonishing.

The experiences kept coming when a couple of days later, Sydney's mother called and said, "They had me write down a bunch of names and they're weird names with strange symbols." She asked her mother to spell them for her and then searched for each one of the names on the internet. She could only find one, it was the name "Ukaooke" which appeared in the book of Genesis in the Swahili language. Google would not translate it, so she couldn't find out what that section of the Bible was referring to.

DRAMSYE

UKAOOKE

ZULAE

OPAZURK

SURSEKÍC

LowLAARUK

PYEOPE

BAYLEZ

EOURPTX

DADAE

ZEPEK

UPALIC

Sydney decided to visit her mother to obtain the names she had channeled but received a lot more information than she expected. Her mother brought out a handful of pictures she drew. They were human/extra-terrestrial-looking people and she had wondered if those were the people her mother communicates with. Beverly explained that she becomes obsessive, sitting down for thirty minutes and drawing these pictures, one after another. She had a strong urge to draw the pictures and it felt really good when she was done; almost like it was a reward. She said she had more than the handful she gave Sydney but couldn't find them all. She was told they are people from other planets and some of the beings are them.

Sydney studied the drawings and came across one that stood out. Not only did some of the human-looking people have cat eyes, but in looking closer, one had eyes that had stars in them. After asking about this being, Sydney was told she was a woman with the name "LGaiai". LGaiai had special bug-like eyes that could see in the dark and she would never need glasses. Sydney was also told that the people in the drawings that have a Merkabah, their symbol which represents the universe, are the biblical people from the Orion Constellation.

Another drawing featured a being the Orions made with pointy ears, a flatter nose, and strange eyelids. He has hair that is in cornrows. His eyes and eyelids are like that of lizards and both the upper and lower eyelids meet and close together. Included was a detail showing this eye. His ears are pointy because it rains a lot where he lives, and it helps protect his ears from water getting in.

Other drawings included the person's name and other strange sayings. There is a man with a beard who appears to be a mountain man which states, "Sharks bite out here in the woods."

Haiai

"STAR LiGHT"

Ronnie Theroux

SHARK'S BITE
OUT HERE
IN THE WOOD'S

The Theologians of Orion

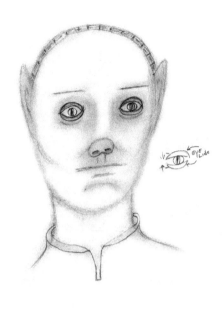

The dreams continued and a month later Sydney had a dream she was outdoors and saw an eye in a triangle high in the sky and it came down closer toward her. She tried to be courageous and stay there but got nervous and went inside the house. She tried to be brave, so she went back outside, and it was gone. The clouds then started moving and formed into a person that looked like an old Mayan person. The clouds in the form of this person came down toward her. She stayed until she got nervous, then went back inside the house, only to come right back out once again and it was gone. She found she was able to manipulate her dream when it became too scary for her when she made herself go back into the house.

Two days later Sydney had a dream of riding in an open-top car with some people and then seeing a bright light above. They all looked to the sky with a bright light on their faces. She said to someone, "Looks like we're going to be taken." And she remembers not being afraid.

Since Sydney did a past life regression, she decided to take her mom to see Barbara Lamb, a well-known regressionist. She was trying to find out more about these people that have contacted them through her Mother. Sydney and her mother were surprised to learn that Barbara had some experiences of her own and stated she was in immediate danger of a poisonous snake right near her. She had no means of escape when her body was lifted and moved several feet away. And when she was put down, it was like she hit the ground running. She believed it was her guardian angel.

Prior to Beverly going under, she was flooded with a lot of information. "Mistakes were made in making us. We don't hear and we don't see. We ignore what they try to tell and show us. We don't do anything about problems until it's too late. Many people are helping with the destruction of mankind. We were their hope, but we are demolishing the hope. We were here to enjoy life, but we're destroying it. Not all beings on every planet are good. You've lost your sense of caring. How you go the extra mile is caring even when you think you can't. They brought people here. They put 12 in Egypt, 12 in North America, 12 in Argentina, and so on. They say man wrote the Bible with their own interpretations. Adam and Eve didn't populate the Earth. People fear things far beyond and don't dissect them to see what they really mean. They put people on Earth to see what would happen. When they give too much information at a time, we cannot process it. We process it bit by bit. People were given free will. They give me messages when I get out of the shower. They are like us, but different, the greys. Their brains are wireless. The grey types are almost human, they have a chip in their brains. They are Retrievers. They come back and take us to retrieve info about us. They are programmed to take us and follow a procedure. They take us to check us out for long-term exposure to pollution. They have no emotion, or they wouldn't do their procedures. They have to put implants in humans to upgrade humans.

After a time, the DNA went out. The greys are prototypes, almost human, no love, no hate. They only do their jobs. The greys did ruin their planet like we are, so they live underground here. They let the robots do the job of abductions being they couldn't take our atmosphere and environment. The robots are prototypes programmed to do certain things. They are a combination of biological material and mechanical apparatus. They absorb food through their skin. I know these messages are true. I don't get these messages all the time, maybe twice per month. I have no background in all of this material. We have more than six senses, but we don't use them. They are trying to save us and also save themselves.

Recently I was out on my front porch and I was shown a picture in my mind of a little girl, about five years old standing next to a very tall man. He was about eight feet tall. He was holding her hand. He had on a double cape like they wore long ago. I was told I had many lifetimes on Earth and I left something important undone when I died. I was never totally satisfied with my life. I need to do it more right and thorough this life. I blew all those six past lives. I didn't do life right."

They finally got around to the regression to explore Beverly's abduction. Beverly got settled in her seat and immediately became relaxed as Mrs. Lamb began the regression. Beverly closed her eyes and began to repeat what was coming to her.

"When I saw the spaceship in 1958, they gave me a message in my mind that said, *"Don't be afraid, we won't hurt you."* We were in the car; my cousin was driving. I looked to my left at her but now I can't move. I don't know what it is – are we in shock? All I think of is flying saucers. We're frozen, not talking.

They're very blunt, so very blunt I believe. It seems I am on the left side of the car. Walking to the house. I'm saying, "Oh my God how can this be?" She's shocked. I am somehow already by the driver's car door. She's getting out of the car. We're quiet. I don't think she's worried about it. She lets the car door go. She wants to get into the house. I see the front yard. We woke up in the driveway. We were just there. I think they just put us back home. They just got us here. We did not drive. I would have remembered that.

We're walking up the steps - I'm still trying to talk; she doesn't want to hear it. It's unusual her mom isn't up waiting for us. We see the object out there, a bit away from us. We see it from her bedroom window, and we knew it was seeing us. As soon as we saw it, they zoomed away. They are aware of us being aware of them. My cousin doesn't want to talk about it. I sense they wanted me to know they are out there. I want to talk about it, but she won't. We went to bed. We didn't close the curtains; we covered our heads under the covers."

The regression was over, and they were all surprised at the information that came before it started and during the regression. It shed light on how Beverly reacted to the experience. They thanked Mrs. Lamb, collected the recording of the regression, and left.

Sydney continued to try and speak to the people who spoke through her mother, but clear communication was hard to achieve as her mother was having a hard time trying to understand everything they were telling her. Sydney decided to give her mind a break for a week to travel, after being invited to the Galapagos Islands by a friend. It was at this point that it seemed like things started coming to her, things she was supposed to experience so she could tell the world. As an odd coincidence, she was heading to the place which was the subject of Charles Darwin's writings on evolution. Sydney began to feel like people were guided in her life to direct her to experience things that would be important to write down and share.

It was Sydney's first morning in Quito, Ecuador, on her way to the Galapagos Islands, and she could see a statue of the Virgin Mary from her hotel window. She and her friend, Jennifer, were picked up by their tour guides and taken to a small airport where they would board a plane to the Galapagos. After the flight, a bus, and two boats they had arrived at their destination, where they planned to stay for three nights.

Sydney and Jennifer spent their time touring three islands, each of them beautiful and teeming with life. She had seen such breathtaking nature on television but found it indescribably stunning to experience it in real life. Their tour guide explained various bird species and how they had evolved one way on one of the islands, and then different on a neighboring one. Sometimes a bird of the same species would have a different length beak on one island versus an island right next to it, due to how it evolved to eat whichever types of nuts were available to that island. Sydney didn't feel like evolution was the best way to describe this occurrence, but couldn't say why. The group made their way on to see tortoises, where again the guide went on to talk about their evolution. For some reason, Sydney's instincts were still telling her something in the information was off, but she didn't dare mention it.

The rest of the trip went without any issues. They saw beautiful birds, sea creatures, and iguanas. She even got to witness a flamingo fly. Once the Galapagos trip was over, they flew back to Quito for two more nights. On the last day of their stay, they did a tour of the Equator line where they got to see how water in a sink would drain in one direction on one side of the equator and the opposite way on the other, all within a couple of feet of one another.

Sydney and Jennifer went to downtown Quito to see the President's house, the Iglesia La Campana church that is decorated in gold leaf and kept in top condition, and some other nearby churches. Sydney was not feeling well but tried to ignore it. A 600-year-old church got her attention; for some reason, she was drawn to it. Some of the local elderly women were lined up along the building, sitting outside of it asking for money. She witnessed two of them having a yelling argument as the rest of the ladies sat in a line against the church all just laughing at them. Sydney found it funny and laughed too, even though she had no idea what they were saying.

While Jennifer was occupied, Sydney decided to go into the church she was drawn to. She found it sad that the church was falling apart. It was very dilapidated, but she found it and its paintings charming. Sydney was still suffering from health issues due to the mold at her previous workplace and was feeling defeated. She went up to the first row on the far-left-hand side and sat next to some of the locals who were praying. After a long two-year battle, she finally prayed for her health. She finally asked for help from God. She had prayed years before but was never sure if it was helpful. This time was different.

CHAPTER 3

Zakaryahan

Upon returning from her trip to Ecuador, Sydney decided to visit her mother again to do another question-and-answer session with the people who spoke telepathically to her mother. She wanted to find out more about who they were and why they had contacted them.

This time she had a list of questions ready. What happened next changed her whole world. Beverly sat down on the couch, and Sydney on a loveseat next to her. She looked at her list and before she could get a word out, her mother began speaking. They began to address Sydney's health issues. She was caught off-guard.

"They have been trying to help you, but you do not heed their signals," Beverly stated.

Beverly continued channeling, "You need to get away from everything because you are making yourself sick, you should be hearing nothing but wind and sand beneath your feet or suffer the consequences."

Then they said, "Flash, flash, flash, flash" as Beverly motioned with her hand.

"What does that mean?" Sydney asked.

"Listen to the signals. We are concerned about you, that you're very affected."

Beverly continued, "We see you getting sicker if you don't take a grip. It's not just the thing you were exposed to you need to get away from, you need to live your own life and not worry about other's problems."

Sydney knew what they meant because her friend at the time was having a lot of personal problems that were becoming hers. Then they stated, "You are on a thin line and need to go to a retreat. You are lucky to have gone as long as you have." At this point, Sydney didn't know what to say because she wasn't prepared to hear these things. She found this a good enough time as any to have all her questions answered, while she had the attention of these people.

"What was the purpose of picking up my mom in 1958?" Sydney started with.

"To give her intelligence."

"Am I a hybrid?"

"You are all hybrids. You all have a part of us. We were all one at one time."

"Because we came from the source?"

"This here was out of desperation. Earth was out of desperation."

"To save people from other planets?"

"Because a planet they were on died because they did the same thing you're doing now."

"Which planet is that?"

"Arachius."

"How are humans being upgraded?"

"You get upgraded telepathically."

Sydney figured these beings interact with souls and spirits, so she asked about her father who died when she was nine.

"Where is my father?"

"Safe."

"Does he visit me?"

"He never left."

"What happens to your family, when you die, do you meet up with them?"

"Not all of them."

Then Beverly paused and said, "Someone wants to talk to you, he says he is your Guardian Angel." Sydney had heard of Guardian Angels, but she never really thought much of them. She had no idea they were real. She sat there in amazement, trying not to freeze with a perplexed look on her face, and said, "What?"

Her mother continued to repeat what she was being told through her.

"I was assigned to you, and I brought you here."

"Was I a walk-in?"

"You were born."

"Does everyone have a guardian angel?"

"Yes, I whispered in your ear long ago, but you did not take heed about your health."

He continued, "You are special, and you need protection more so than anyone."

Sydney sat listening intently. Well, that was a strong statement, she thought.

"Why do I need protection?"

"You're very special, that's why."

"Is it something you can't tell me?"

"Too much to fathom. In time. You have to learn lessons before you get more. Because with your lessons, you will find more questions."

"What is special about me?"

"You."

"What is your name?"

"Zakaryahan."

Sydney asked him to spell it and he did. She asked him about the dream she had with the grey alien, and he said, "That was me."

"Are you a grey?" Sydney asked.

He said, "No."

"What was the cassette tape sound in my mind?"

"I put it there in trying to stimulate you, preparing you for your next download. For your next upgrade. You will go through some lessons in the future."

"I felt it and I heard it and I felt great for three days, confident and strong," Sydney replied.

Sydney couldn't stop now, she had to continue asking questions. She would ask all night if it was possible if Zakaryahan would allow it.

"Is Valiant Thor, the man who came from Venus, a real person?"

"He's Half and half."

"A hybrid?"

"Yes and no."

"What is he?"

"He's not in our galaxy."

"Is Omnec Onec the lady who says she's from Venus – is it true?"

"Yes, she is. Treat her kindly."

"I would like to know who I was before this life, in a past life."

"Down the line. You need to learn a lot of things before things are told to you."

"Who is God? Is he a source of light energy like we think he is?"

"I'll put it to you this way if you didn't have a God who would you have? In a time of need, who would you ask for?"

"Is there one God?"

"No, there are a lot of Gods, but there is only one God, God."

"Are you a physical person?"

"Yes. I am able to be where I am and to be with you all the time by transcending."

"What do you look like?"

"I am here, right behind you and you don't need to talk loudly."

"He's behind me?"

"Yes, he is always with you," said Beverly.

Sydney's guardian angel continued with the question about what he looked like.

"I have dark hair, blue eyes, and I am seven and a half feet tall."

"I thought the tall people were the creator Gods, is that true?"

"Not true. There are a lot of tall people. You don't have to be that tall to be a creator or biblical. It's who you are and how you present yourself that makes you big."

"Am I part of these biblical people?"

"You're special."

Sydney's mom continued to recite what Zakaryahan was saying to her, "I have my thumb on you. You held things in and just bared through things."

Sydney thought to herself that those words rang so true.

"How old are you?"

"Ninety-Nine years."

"How old do you look?"

"Forty."

"How long do you live?"

"As long as they allow me to."

"Do you have children?"

"Yes, two, ages seven and eight."

"What are their names?"

"Their names are Tilian and Raha."

"Are you married?"

"No, I have a partner."

"Is it true that if we don't change our pollution in the next eighty years, it is going to be irreversible?"

"It will be downhill - deformities."

"What is my IQ?"

"It is high."

"If you could put a number to it, what would it be?"

"One hundred sixty, but you don't use it to its full capacity."

"I read the Bible when I was young every night."

"I know."

"I stopped reading the Bible because something came to me that told me that the Bible is the word of man and not God. Did you put that in my ear?"

"Yes."

"It's not because the Bible is bad, it's not. I just didn't understand at the time that even though God didn't write the Bible, he inspired the writings. God gave the Ten Commandments, but it meant more than the ten things and it was for the people to expand on, to teach the word of God."

"As a little girl, I felt like I wasn't from here like I didn't want to be here."

"None of you were from here."

"I felt like I didn't want to be here."

"Because you're not happy. You had an inability to speak."

"Yes, I was very shy, I didn't like people."

"You saw too much and you ran with that. You took the bad and ran with it. You should have picked some good out of it. You had a lot of bad negativity from people that was falling on you."

Zakaryahan continued, "All of these little sayings mean a lot if people would only read it out loud and listen. They were made up for a reason hoping people would understand better."

"When I was going through a really hard time, I was laying down trying to take a nap and I was very stressed when a voice came into my mind that told me everything was going to be okay. Was that you?"

"It was part of me."

"Parts of you and parts of a collective group of people?"

"Yes, you have a lot of them around you."

"Do we all have that?"

"Yes, it's a good thing. They don't see the bad in you. You need not look back on the past at the bad things, you need to look forward to the good things because you will never get out of the past."

"Did the Annunaki have slaves here to mine gold?

"Not the ones here. There were others that went to Earth from other planets to do that kind of bidding."

"I heard how we originated here that adults were brought here or seeds planted here."

"Adults were brought here already seeded."

"I know how to change my dreams, that if it's going down a scary path, I can change it.

"He said you need to do that now," Beverly chimed in.

"Are there bases on the moon?"

"Yes, motherships."

"Does our government know about it?"

"Yes."

"Do we have bases there?"

"No."

"I'd like to go on a spaceship ride."

"You are due."

"Do I have any special abilities?"

"Yes, but you haven't found all of them yet. Not all of them, you found some good ones."

"Do I have any other special abilities, such as healing?"

"Not yet, in a way you do. With the person you are as far as being really quiet and the way you present yourself to people and the words you say is what comforts people and that's where you're healing."

"Lately I have been feeling warmth on my face. What is that?"

"You are coming alive, knowing."

"Have you been trying to wake me up for a long time?"

"Yes, people don't hear or see."

"Are you funny?"

"Yes, you have to be. You can't understand without a personality-plus."

"Who are the people my mother draws?"

"People who help."

"Are those people who talk to her?"

"Some."

"How about the names channeled to her?"

"Those are real."

"They are biblical people from where we are from. They're like our forefathers, but they are alive."

"They watch over them," said Beverly.

"Who's them?"

"Him, your Guardian Angel. They watch over all of us," Beverly explained.

"He is from what planet?"

"Ortanium? Oh, it's a funny one," said Beverly.

"Has he ever been to earth in a physical body?"

"No. Telepathy."

"Is he in a spaceship somewhere?"

"No."

"Is he on a planet right now?"

"Here. He is on earth right now. He's with you," Beverly answered.

"He's with me all the time?"

"More so than ever."

"Because of my health?"

"Because you're listening."

"He's trying to spell something for me. O-r-t-i-z-a-n... O-r-t-r-a-z-a-n.... O-r-t-a-z-a-n. I think it's the second one because that's what he said first and was saying it with the *R* after the *T*. He is spelling the planet he is from," Beverly said.

Sydney changes the subject, "About the pyramids in Egypt, were the blocks levitated into place?"

"No, they were rolled onto lumber and piled by the slaves."

"And they used the pulley system?"

"Yes, and we cut the stone. You can only do so much for the people, or it would make them weak. Use your own mind to judge. There were many slaves and when slaves died, lots more came."

"Where is the Ark of the Covenant?"

"It is all over the world. It was made of wood, so it disintegrated."

"Why not do another mass sighting as they did in Arizona in 1997?"

"It would cause mass hysteria."

Zakaryahan continued to tell Sydney that she felt lost from the time she was left by accident by her mom when she was young and how she needed to let go of that. Sydney knew exactly what he was talking about.

Sydney spoke up, "When I was a young girl, about five, I was being babysat along with my sister overnight. We were staying in a two-story white house with a white wooden fence. When I went to bed that night, I felt a presence so I pulled the covers over my head. Was that a ghost?"

"That was me," said Zakaryahan.

Sydney didn't expect that answer because she assumed it was a ghost since her sister said she saw a ghost in that house. She just offered that information a year prior without Sydney even telling her that she felt something was there. So, her guardian angel was at this strange house watching over her. She felt the presence strongly.

Sydney asked him about when she went to her first UFO conference and had the aura around her that the two hotel workers noticed. He said he put protective energy around her. He thought she needed it. He said it wasn't so much for protection, but power. Sydney replied that she could understand that because she was venturing into a strange new world by herself. This blanket of power made her feel confident. Sydney told him that she felt that throughout her life. He said more people would feel that if they would only listen.

Zakaryahan said the people we channel are biblical people from Orion. He said he is also associated with Orion, and he is part human. Zakaryahan then asked Sydney to look up the Orion Constellation and said, "You will be amazed."

Sydney moved to the table where the computer was and looked it up. Then she asked, "What is it you wish us to see?"

"You have to seek to find. Look to Orion, it holds many answers."

"Can you tell me what the negative forces are on the planet?"

"Too many."

"Is it the reptilians that are controlling things?"

"No, but they're trying to."

"Grey aliens? Good or bad or both?"

"Both. It all depends on how they're programmed."

Sydney mentioned a time when she was on a redeye flight and saw something explode in the sky. It looked like a shooting star going very slow, down across the sky, then there was a flash of light and two skip marks, followed by another explosion.

"That was one of ours, we call him a Sender, he's like a scout."

"Was it a grey in the ship?"

"Yes. There's a lot of different greys."

"People here have cataloged fifty-seven types. Are there more than that?"

"Yes."

"Did the Senders crash their ship?"

"Yes. It got into the atmosphere and it happens all the time, people don't realize that. We're not perfect, but there's turbulence in the atmosphere and we didn't expect it and it threw him off course and it burned him up. It's one of ours that does our seeking, he's our scout, and we have a lot of them. Some of the ships get too close to the atmosphere without putting up their shield in time."

"Did he die?"

"Way under."

"What does that mean? Way under the ground? Does his spirit live on?"

"No, because he has a program. They don't have souls. His memory only is what we program them to be."

Sydney asked about the dream she had of Jesus and asked if he really came to visit her.

"Yes. It was the deepest love you ever experienced and that you will never get from any relationship there."

This hit home for Sydney because that's what she was telling her friends and family, those same words. Our guides, our angels, hear and see what we do. "You are very inquisitive!" said Zakaryahan.

Zakaryahan brought up many things about Sydney that no one else would know. She believed he did this so that she would believe this was indeed real. He told her that she kept things in and was a silent person. He said she would get very angry, and it made it hard for people to get close to her. Sydney knew what this meant – that it had to do with bad people and being treated so horribly.

Sydney changed the subject to have more of her questions answered.

"Have I been upgraded?"

"You keep getting upgraded; you get it telepathically."

Sydney was astonished by the conversation she was having. Her mother said these people don't normally do this for anyone, to allow them to talk to their guardian angel or communicate with humans this extensively. They felt she needed it because she was going through a hard time. Sydney decided to ask her final questions.

"Is our theory of evolution correct?"

"Humans have it all wrong about evolution," Zakaryahan answered.

"Are we manipulated to fit our environment?"

"Yes."

Zakaryahan left the conversation to let the Orions answer a few questions for them.

"I am wondering why my Guardian Angel said that he lives as long as they allow him to. Who are they?" Sydney asked.

Beverly answered, "It's them, the Orions."

"He earns his way," the Orions spoke.

"Is he doing a good job?" Sydney asked.

"He won't know until he earns his way. He has rules to live by. He can only go out on a limb so far and then he has to let you fall so you can learn, or you will never learn. We would be hurting you if we didn't let you fall."

Beverly was getting tired and wanted to end the communication. Sydney was still in shock and wanted to say one last thing. She looked her mother in the face and told them that they loved them. She was on cloud nine and could not believe what had happened. She was not prepared to hear from her Guardian Angel. There's got to be more to why this is happening, she thought. It appears they heard her prayers.

Sydney decided she needed to leave even though she didn't want to. She was on a high from such an amazing experience but knew it made her mother very tired. She said it would take her breath away. Sydney left and planned to stay at a friend's house for a few days on a beach, just like the Orions told her.

Three days later and Sydney did exactly what they told her. She put her remaining things in storage and went to the beach to feel the wind in her face and the sand under her feet. It was what she needed. She left the things that were bringing her down. It was there that she was to unwind, get some rest, and try to recover from her health issues.

While walking the beach and perusing a Farmer's Market, Sydney's mother called to tell her that her special friends had a long and important message for her. Beverly recited the message she had written down, and Sydney's jaw dropped to the floor.

• • • •

"You were a challenge. We had to bring you to Earth because you were too different and you couldn't live in our world. We wanted you to be happy and prosperous, so we chose Earth as the planet best suited for you. You were our experiment and we still watch over you. You need to open your eyes and listen to your Earth. We gave you the chance to all live in peace and harmony. You do not think beyond your nose. The Ten Commandments is all you need to go by to live a good life. Remember if you didn't have a God to look upon for help and fulfillment what would you do. You would be lost.

We want to help, but from afar. No way could we socialize, reason being we are too different in our bodies, our way of thinking, our way of living. Marriage would be like a giraffe, living and consorting with an ape. We would be creating a new strange and different world, a world that should be placed on another planet. This is what happened before. We took part of ourselves and developed you. Through time and error, we created you. We wanted you all the same, but different."

8-13

II

YOU WERE A CHALLENGE.
WE HAD TO bRING YOU TO
EARTH BECAUSE YOU WERE TOO
diFFERENT AND YOU Couldn't
LIVE IN OUR WORLd.
WE WANTED YOU TO bE
happy AND prosPEROUS, SO WE
chose EARTH AS THE planeT
bEST SUiTED FOR YOU. YOU
WERE OUR EXPERIMENT AND
WE STILL WATCH OVER YOU —
YOU NEED TO OPEN YOUR
EYES AND liSTEN TO YOUR
EARTH. WE gAVE YOU THE
ChANCE TO ALL LIVE IN
PEACE AND hARMONY. YOU
do NOT THINK BEYOND YOUR
NOSE — THE TEN COMMAND-
MENTS IS ALL YOU NEED TO
go by TO liVE A GOOD LiFE.
Remember IF You didn't
hAVE A GOD TO LOOK UPON
FOR HELP AND FulfullMENT
WHAT Would you do.... You
would bE LOST —

They want To help, but FROM
A FAR —
No WAY could WE SOCIALIZE
REASON being, WE ARE To
diFFERENT iN OUR bodies,
OUR WAY OF THINKING, OUR WAY
OF LiViNG —
    MARRiAGE would be liKE
A GiRAFF, LiViNG AND con-
SORTiNG with AN ApE
    WE would be CREATING A
NEW STRANGE AND DIFFERENT
WORld.
    A WORLD THAT SHOUld be
placeD ON ANOtheR plANET.
    This is WHAT HAppENED
BEFORE.
    WE TooK pART of OURSElves
AND DEVELOpED yOU. ThRU
TIME AND ERROR WE CREATED
yOU. WE WANTED yOU ALL
THE SAME, BUT DiFFERENT—

CHAPTER 4

Them

The Orions are the people who are God's right hands. God placed humans on the planet, but there weren't enough of them. God then created an advanced race and taught them to create. It was the Orions, and they cloned humans for God and placed groups of twelve different cultures in various places on the Earth.

As the Orions explained it to Sydney,

"Adam and Eve had two children. How can you make more people on the planet if all you have is a mother, a father, and two brothers? It doesn't happen. And that is where the help came in."

The Orions then began to put one hundred people of different races in various places on the earth. It was an experiment, the first of its kind, and that's why the Earth is so special. That is why so much attention is put on Earth, and why Jesus visited this planet and no others.

The communication with the Orions was still in its infancy when Sydney sat down with her mother to ask more questions. This is when they learned who they are.

"Are you creators of the first humans?"

"Yes, but we had help."

"Who did you have help from?"

"God."

"Is Orion the place of original creation?"

"Yes. Creation of all things."

"Are you the Anunnaki?"

"No, but there were Anunnaki that came from Orion."

Beverly spoke, "Their group starts with a T, like T-r-i. They are spelling for me. Theologians. They are called Theologians."

Sydney paused and said, "Mom, do you realize what you have?" Sydney continued with her questioning.

"The people from Orion who created the original humans, are they still alive or long gone?"

"They are gone. We can live forever, but we don't want to live forever."

"What is your group's purpose?"

"To preserve peace and balance of the worlds."

"When you communicate with us, use both heart and mind. One is not good without the other."

"Was there an advanced group that altered humans after they were brought to Earth?"

"Yes, it was us. We want to keep part of us in you, but after years it (DNA) gets thinned out."

"So then are we are upgraded by them to keep some of their DNA in us?"

"Yes, if we wanted, we could program you like we do the retrievers, the greys."

"What is the purpose of keeping their DNA in us?"

"It keeps us closer, and we know who you are, that you belong to our group."

Beverly explained, "It's like a chip, so they know who we are."

"Do the other advanced people from other planets put their own people here on Earth?"

"Yes, but about 55% of the earth's population has Orion DNA. The rest are the other advanced races, but we watch over all of you."

"How far in the future can you see?"

"It's not really the future that we look into. It's common sense. We have a wider common sense."

"What is an average IQ for you?"

"That's hard to answer."

"Are the people that my mom draws, are they pictures of you?"

"Some are and some are from other planets."

"Do you look human like we do?"

"Yes, but different. We are taller, stronger mentally and physically."

"Do you live in buildings as we do?"

"Kind of. We're partly in the Earth and in rocks. It keeps us cool when it's hot, keeps us warm when it's cold."

"How do you travel within your planet?"

"We don't tire."

Beverly spoke, "I see a vision of them uplifting, like maybe they have something in their feet like they have energy in the feet. I see the body going like they have something in the feet."

"Do they live in a different dimension?"

Beverly answered, "He said no, it's just that they're so far away that it would seem that way. They don't age like us."

Sydney realized her mother mentioned "he" which she hadn't heard her say before. She was talking about a certain person.

"Wait a minute, who is HE?" Sydney asked.

Beverly said, "He said his name is Zentuse with an 'e' on the end. They are showing me an upside-down 'V,' with the collective people in the V and Zentuse being at the point. He is the leader or the main person from which the communication comes. I hear mumbling from thousands of people and then a voice from Zentuse."

Beverly continued, "They're now showing me a picture of a tall man leaning over and talking to a child. That's to show that they are the tall people, and we are the children. He, Zentuse is wearing a cape, and it looks like Sherlock Holmes' cape. They wear old clothes like that."

"Since you are so important, how do you stay protected?"

"We have our ways."

"Are you more like perfect people?"

"Yes, we lived and learned."

"Do you create planets?"

"No, we took the souls of the dead and put them on another planet. It's been going on for years and years. The ones that already were there that had gone through reincarnation, had babies, but those babies were from good souls from Earth. We are doing the same thing with other planets because of overflow of souls."

"How are planets made?"

"A magnet has a lot to do with it."

"Do you interact with God?"

"Yes and no."

"Jesus?"

"All in one."

"What is a typical day like for you?"

"Everyone has their duties, they do them and then we rest. Very important, rest. We make each day count. Every day we climb the ladder, one rung at a time. Everybody works together.

We get it done, no matter how big or small. Everybody depends on everybody; you can't break that chain."

"What do you do for entertainment?"

"We all just gather when we have the time, and we have free concerts."

"What kind of music is it?"

"Sweet music, relaxing, comfortable."

"Is it like classical music?"

"Yes, like elevator music."

"Are there any other types of music?"

"We do, but it's all soothing. There's a great big crater and these people that play the instruments get down in the hole. The music comes up and you can hear it all over. We all stand at the top."

"What kind of instruments do they have?"

"To you, it would be funny, strange-looking, different."

"How many people are on your planet?"

"Hundreds of thousands."

"Do you have bad people on your planet?"

"No, we take them and put them on other planets."

"What kind of animals do you have?"

"Similar to yours, but different."

"Are you able to leave your physical body and become a light body?"

"When we leave our planet in our ships, it is kind of like that. We do get like that, but you wouldn't understand it."

"When they travel through wormholes, their bodies dematerialize then they come back together again. Their bodies do a split-atoms thing," said Beverly.

"We can do that with your body by shooting a beam at you, then take you through a solid object like a wall or ceiling of a house. That's what our greys do."

"Can you tell us something about your ships, how they're made?"

"Our gyro is made of crystals and magnets and it's intricately balanced. When we travel in ships, we don't feel G forces."

"What are your clothes like?"

"Everything on our planet is made easy, everything is made simple. Everything is made from good things and good fibers."

"You mentioned you have a tree of life. Please explain that."

"We have something we call our Tree of Life. It is a tree that emits a sap that is very healing. One of our scientists has to monitor it and give it out to our people who need it. We also had a ball, a ball that was very sacred and would only be given to someone very deserving. You hold it and it absorbs into your skin, and it makes you feel good all over. First to the feet, then to the heart, and then the head. It's very sacred, it wraps around you, and your body is enveloped in the feeling. It's on the Earth somewhere and is only for hierarchy, like Gandhi. Gandhi had it."

"Can you tell us something else about yourselves that is different from us?"

"We have healthier blood than you do. We're tall and lanky. Our heads are a bit bigger and rounder than yours. Our language is like Arabic with Greek symbols. We don't like language that goes way out. We are very short and to the point. We like something that speaks right now."

"What do you eat?"

"We are vegetarian. It's brain food. Cutting out a lot of the meat would be best. Add more fruit and vegetables to your dinner with smaller pieces of meat. You should put more vegetables and fruit on the table."

"How is the health of people on your planet?"

"We don't have a lot of health issues. We don't have cancer and all the problems on your planet, and we don't get colds.

we endure traveling from planet to planet."

"Is there a cure for the common cold?"

"There will never be a cure for the common cold. It cleanses your body."

"Why do we have different blood types?"

"Because you're different people, with different problems and that's what makes the world go around. It would be an uninteresting place to live. You would have no reason for hope."

"Early in your evolution did you have buildings and vehicles like us?"

"No, we started out like you did, very similar but more pure. We live off the land, we make everything count. We try to live as simple lives as we can. We live off the land because we don't like pollution; the more extravagant life you have, the more pollution you create. We live simple lives. You want too much, too fast and you don't take care of what you have. You destroy things as fast as you make them. You have no respect for the Earth or other planets. We learn to breathe as you say breathe. We have our times of laughter and times of peace, but we have to always in the time of peace and resting, have you and the other planets in the back of our mind. We are blunt, with a dry sense of humor."

"Did you have vehicles as we did?"

"No. They come off the ground."

"How is it that one of your people can suddenly appear, like a Guardian Angel who steps in to protect someone?"

"We have to step through a dimension. It's like a sheet of something, like going through a cloud. The Guardian Angels appear through thought, need, and urgency. They have to go faster than what they are stepping through and it doesn't hurt anything on them. It's like when we travel in our ships and our bodies split atoms. The same thing happens when we go through a dimension."

"Your Guardian Angel did that for you before, also on an occasion recently that you were not aware of. When you were driving at night, Zakaryahan had to jump into a car that was going to hit you on the freeway. We felt we needed to protect you from that, because we couldn't see you dealing with that hardship at that time."

"I am aware of when that was, it was about six weeks ago. I heard the screeching of tires and I looked around to see where it was coming from. I thought I was going to be hit and braced myself."

"How do they know to appear in a certain location?"

"We have all kinds of different coordinates that we've had for millions of years, and we know where to go. There are stairways to all the planets. When we go through a dimension in our ships, we have to go through it sideways, very quickly because if our gyro becomes unlevel, we will crash. When our ships enter the ocean, we have to get sideways and hit the water at an angle as well. We have to slice through it."

"Wow that's amazing, on another subject, can you tell us about how the first physical body was made?"

"In Labs, just like you have labs. Kind of the same way, but each person is made different. Humans make clones. A lot of people that come back are reincarnated into another body, into that baby. A baby that is born takes the soul of someone who has already died. Some people cannot leave the Earth."

"Why can't they leave the Earth?"

"They either didn't do life right or they didn't finish. If you don't feel finished, you cannot go on. You can't die and rest in peace."

"At what point in time is the soul brought into the person?"

"When it's in the mother. It just is."

"Some people think we had a soul agreement before coming into the body, is that correct?"

"No. There were a lot of agreements, but it wasn't that."

"What kind of agreements?"

"A lot but you never stuck to any of them."

"Is it because we forgot once we came into our body?"

"You didn't care."

"Is there another group who is in charge of the creation of animals?"

"No. All the same, from Orion."

"Is that where God resides in Orion?"

"He is everywhere."

"Was it God who created the first person?"

"He really created everyone and then he gave them the will and knowledge to others who also created. Now it has gone rampant, like a bunch of rabbits. The more people, the more pollution you create."

"Who was this first person?"

"They're all pieces of Jesus. Their DNA. In the likeness of God, so Jesus is a likeness of God."

"Do you call the constellation of Orion a name different from what we call it?"

"No."

"Where did evil come from?"

"From within, from wanting something so strong that nothing else mattered. A lot of people should not have been born. Like something in their brain malfunctioned."

"Did the Earth collide with another planet during its formation?"

"It had a lot of meteor storms, big meteors. Meteors were a good thing, that's how the lakes were formed, and volcanoes were good because they pushed the Earth up to form mountains."

"Why don't we remember our life before coming into our bodies?"

"Because you would be dealing with issues from your past lives."

"Is there such thing as The Big Bang?"

"The universe was created. God created the universe."

"Is there more than one universe?"

"Lots, yes. Universes inside of universes."

"I have always felt different. Who am I?"

"You are lost and you need to find yourself."

"Who am I in the spirit world?"

"Just a good person trying to do right."

"My guardian angel said he brought me here. Does that mean he brought my soul into my body?"

"It stems from the DNA. He upgrades your DNA."

"What is God? How do you describe God?"

"All-knowing, everything good, infinity, everlasting, ever-loving, ever-caring, always there."

"Is God male or female?"

"Male."

"How did God come to exist?"

"Because he is. If there was no God there would be no you, there would be nothing."

"What percentage of Earth's population gets upgrades?"

"Everybody at a certain time. We need to keep the DNA in there because there is another species on Earth and that's how we keep you straight."

"What do you look like?"

"About the same as you. We always have to wear long sleeves."

"Are there some people who have blue skin as I've read about?"

"It looks blue, but it's grey. Real thin."

"Are you gods?"

"We are not gods. If you want to call us gods, call us scientific gods. We are less biblical and more scientific. We only go for the things two and two, the environment and living; about saving people and planets. You have all of the literature there that you need about whatever you're worried about, or you want to know about. You have to read and figure out what you want to believe. Just like different religions. God gave you your free will, but we don't like the way you're taking the free will and terrorizing the planet, and then it goes onto another planet."

"We are less biblical and more scientific."

"How do you track time periods?"

"We are so far ahead of you, it makes us feel dumb. It's like you not knowing Greek and you only know English and they throw this letter at you and tell you to read it. We have to decipher every single thing, all the millions of things that you have there; the way you add, subtract, how you say things, and why you do things. We are completely different than that, we are on the other end of that, underneath that. We don't do things the way you do them. It makes us dumb because we don't understand why you do what you do because when we put you on the Earth, you were clean. You had to learn, so what you learned was totally different than what we already knew because we already had the knowledge and we had everything we need. When you were put on Earth there was nothing, there was only fruits and vegetation."

"What about where you live, what is that like?"

"We can slide something away from some holes in the caves and let light in every day but only for a certain time then we shut it. We can't put it on a timer, because we don't know when it's going to be a good day for that. We don't have knick-knacks or things like that. We have cubbies in our rooms in our caves. You would not be able to figure out how to get into it."

"They're saying their caves look like straws with a weave made of oats and hay and mud. They have to layer it; you have to know which one to layer because some of them will really cook. With a straw on the top, mud and straw on the top and mix it in," Beverly explained.

"You should see our sunflowers. They're giant," the Orions added.

God gave the Orions the job to "preserve peace and balance of the worlds." They put humans on the planet, and they still protect and watch over us. They are the ones referred to as "The Watchers". They know everything that is going on here. They manage our souls. They hear our prayers. They put us through lessons. They can check in on us at any time by reading the imprint on our souls. They deliver our karma. When we die, they direct our soul to its next incarnation.

The Orions are physical people, and they live underground on their planet. They are over seven feet tall; they fly in spaceships and use wormholes to travel through. They don't need rest as we do, they are always working but when they do have their day of rest, they use it to enjoy soothing music. They are the descendants of the forefathers who populated the Earth with all the different races. They also had a lot of different races and cultures on their planet thousands of years ago, but because of interbreeding, they all became one. They were sad for this to happen, and they hope that Earth will keep its different cultures.

The communication with them isn't perfect because English is not their first language. It is also rare for this group of people from Orion to contact people on the planets. The reason is that they have the greys and the other advanced people to do that for them. A lot of times they use old words because they can't keep up with our language and how it's constantly changing. But out of desperation, they have finally come forward because the messages from the others are not working. They've come forward to tell us how it all works and where we came from. They gave Sydney and her mother information that no one else had so that they would be the ones to wake people up. Their most important message has to do with the environment.

They are the ones who put us here, the ones who put all the vegetation on the planet and animals; everything you need to live. Everything in certain places to balance the world. It was all planned and the Earth was prepared for humans. Part of the preparation was done by directing a large meteor to Earth to kill off the dinosaurs so that there would be a resource for man. The grey beings do the job for them by picking up people and taking samples since they can't come here or they would die.

They run all of the planets and speak telepathically to many other advanced people on multiple planets. And that is the reason they don't care for trivial chatting because they have much more important things to do. They prefer to only communicate with scientists.

They still make new species of plants and animals and things and drop them off on Earth. They said they wanted to make a plant that looks like a hand, but that it would be too telling. However, they put many things on the Earth that would have you scratching your head, but no one questions it.

These people that watch over us know everything we do. They drop in and see us, and they can review your soul imprint which is like a recording of your life. They know if you've been bad or good, but they don't check in during your private times.

CHAPTER 5

A Sick Earth

The next time Sydney planned a visit with her mother, her friend Mark wanted to call and ask questions to the Orions about the environment. Sydney came to realize the environmental crisis was the focus of her purpose on Earth. The Orions told her that we have until 2076 to be exact and after that time, the pollution will be irreversible. So once they sat down at her mother's table, they called Mark who asked the questions. The first subject was the nuclear accident at Fukushima.

"When did the leak from Fukushima reach the U.S. West Coast?" Mark asked.

"Three months after the accident. Your government knew right away."

"Are you helping us with Fukushima?"

"Yes, but something is blocking the avenues to helping. Too many things. We can only do so much so fast. In due time."

"Will people die on the U.S. coast because of it?"

"Yes, the weak – down the line."

"Should we stay out of the oceans?"

"No. Everything is in front of your face, and you don't see it. You need to go backward. The radiation is already in your vegetables, fruits, and milk."

"Should we stop consuming these things?"

"No, your body will filter it out, but the weak will suffer for a long time and finally succumb. The ocean cleanses itself, it filters itself out. The Earth is fighting back because of you, because you're killing it. The ocean will absorb it."

"Will it be cured anytime soon?"

"No."

"Will many more on the West Coast die?"

"Yes."

"What can we do to not be affected?"

"Not much you can do, stay as healthy as you can. The sickness will take more lives down the line."

"Will this cause thyroid issues?"

"Yes, that's the main one."

"Will half a lemon before each meal help?"

"Yes, anything that cleanses will help. Your body will be a filter."

"What about the hole in the atmosphere? People say it's from climate change from pollution."

"We will say a little of it may affect it, but the severe changes in weather fix that issue. It repairs itself. If it didn't, you wouldn't have cold freezing seasons, only hot burning ones. It's been going on for millions of years. You are only measuring a couple hundred years of a planet that is billions of years old. Think about it. Your government is going about it the wrong way."

The Orions continued with other issues:

"Brazil is cutting down too many trees, ruining the atmosphere because of the trees, ruining the balance of nature. People need to get back to their virtues, patience is one of them. If humans in the state they are now were to come to our planet, they would immediately start ruining our planet because you made yours that way. You are killing the planet and atmosphere which affects the universe. You need to plant more trees and foliage to absorb the impurities. As it is now, the radiation is already in your fruits and vegetables and cow's milk. You will become immune to the radiation, but a lot of people will get sicker before they get better. The weak and the old will die.

If you don't stop polluting and taking care of things right now, you're going to end up killing the natural filter that you have on the Earth. You will start choking the Earth off to a point it won't be able to grow anything. The oceans are getting so polluted, the natural seaweeds and breathing organisms are going to get chopped off."

"You are killing the planet and atmosphere which affects the universe."

"Will the plants become radioactive themselves?" Mark asked.

"They are going to help absorb. Once you do all the planting, we are going to help. We are going to send something down to neutralize the vegetation, but you need to have the vegetation planted first and that takes a long time. We send down neutralizing rain as we have done before. You call it the red rain."

Beverly added, "That was them sending the red rain down. Now they're trying to inject the red rain into the fish and the sea. They're like amoeba, so they will absorb impurities. It's an experiment they're putting in different places and they spread it over India."

"Can you help us with the radiation?"

"We are trying on our end. It just got so out of hand. We couldn't predict what was going to happen in Japan. The Japanese put the cart before the horse. They don't speculate what CAN happen and whether it WILL happen. There is always that one element that sets it off like earthquakes and tsunamis. People just walk around in a cloud. When you have more pollution, you will get more storms because the Earth is fighting back trying to purify itself. In doing so it causes the release of bad bacteria. One thing creates another and another, like a domino effect. Money is destroying people's minds and relationships; they base their lives on money. It's good to think about the future, but if that's all you think about, it's a bad thing because you do bad things to get it. The companies don't care about the environment, just money. Your government has destroyed people in more ways than one. The Earth is a living organism, and it cleanses itself through natural disasters, but you are taxing it too much with your pollution."

Beverly took a turn to speak for herself, "They don't always answer my questions but when they do, they just send them to me. They send me a paragraph or three or four words or they flash pictures in my mind, and I have to figure it out. They will be talking about where you can find things that are going to help us and they say *it's all about the ocean*. You see I don't understand that. That's all they give me. They give me bits and pieces of words and they think I understand. Many cures are in the ocean, and we are killing the ocean. It's 50% polluted.

They relay to me constantly to the point it really worries me. They are always saying that we do not listen, we do not hear, we do not see, we do not use all our senses; like we turn our back on the truth instead of going out and doing what we need to do. We base our lives on triviality. They do not like the trivial questions unless it pertains to something very important or it's going to be really big. They don't want to socialize with us, they love us to death, but they know it would never work.

They don't expect us to fly to their planet and vacation. It's not going to happen, and they don't want that. They're only here to help us because in helping us, it's helping them. We are creating so many disasters that are affecting other planets. And what planets are not affected now, will be affected later. It will be in the atmosphere and the planets are closer than you think as far as poisonous gasses getting into the air and traveling. The Earth is like a burning stove that never quits."

"If enough people regularly send heartfelt love to Fukushima, could it transmute the radioactive substance into a safe substance? What do the Orions say about that?" Mark asked.

"It does send out a lot of good vibrations, it will absorb a lot, but the people on Earth need to stop, look and think and hear things. They do not take the time to listen to the Earth. They need to plant more vegetation, a lot of vegetation so that it will absorb, and will absorb a lot of all the bad things that are in your air. Dealing with the Brazil that has so much to do with what is out in your air and all the vegetation that is being cut down has caused so many problems that the Earth is fighting back."

"And what I guess they mean is that we are to be engulfed. A lot of people are going to be engulfed. I don't know what that means. Everyone is going to be put in shock so that maybe they will listen, and they will hear because people don't. They tend to leave everything to everyone else to do. Love is something that we all know and should abide by, and it does help. But with the vegetation, we need to plant a lot of succulents, trees, shrubs, anything that absorbs bad things that float around our Earth," said Beverly.

"You need to try to get your government to listen to you, you the people. But you can't just always rely on them. You need to go out and you need to do what you have to do. You have to convince these people of what's happening; you are killing the earth; you are killing yourself and you are killing us," said the Orions.

"You are killing the Earth, you are killing yourself and you are killing us."

Sydney and her mother sat there looking each other in the eye. They felt stunned, humbled, and shaken, to say the least. "Wow," they said simultaneously, with tears in their eyes.

Beverly continued channeling, "They are begging us to please, please think about what you're doing, and people don't - they don't think."

"They think everything is going to be alright but we're here to tell you we're not alright, you're not alright, the Earth is not alright. The Earth right now is fighting back, and I don't think people can see. They don't see, they don't believe, they don't want to hear. They just turn their back, and they leave it for somebody else to do. It can't be that way. The Earth is sick," said the Orions.

"We're here to tell you we're not alright, you're not alright, the Earth is not alright."

"Is the sea life dying?" asked Mark, who had been sitting and listening in silence.

"It's not dead yet, but there is a blanket, a thick film from oil floating over the top and the sea urchins can't breathe. The ships have a lot to do with that. You need to knock down machinery plants and go back to making things by hand. It's going to get to a point where you won't be able to swim in the ocean or eat anything from the ocean. Everybody always leaves it to the other guy to fix and it never gets fixed. By 2076 to be exact, if you don't start now to clean up, you won't even exist. It will all be downhill from there."

"How do we awaken mankind to something that is not always consistent and repeatable? In other words, alternate dimensions. To things we can't prove, scientists, and so on. How do we do that?" Asked Mark.

"You need to get more scientists together. You need to get a TV station that shows them examples of what has been done to the Earth, pictures, stories, and people continuing bad things. It's something you have to continue. We've been trying to help you, but again, people do not use the senses that were given to them and if they were to open them up, mankind has got to do the initial saving. We can be there only to pick you up and we can send some things to you to help, but the initial is you. You need to know the avenues you have. You must learn to use them.

It's one person at a time, convincing people, on the computer; you need to show them the truth. Your government is blind, and the reason is that they're overwhelmed. They start on one thing, and they end up having to do thousands of other things and they push it aside and your government isn't always true. You must find important people, listening people. Talk to your local public broadcasting system."

Beverly continued her channeling, "They showed me a vision of the U.S. engulfed in a gas. They said this is our future, and the ones being affected are parts of Canada, Mexico, and the U.S. This is what they see in the future, and they said one little thing can spark it. After that, it will singe everything: fruits, vegetables, trees, foliage, and people. Half of all the people in the Americas will be harmed by it. It will happen a long time from now. They said it was built-up combustion. Pollution is the cause; the factories' emissions."

"To help with the radiation, you need to plant a lot of trees, shrubs, and succulents. And you need to get the word out so that others will do the same. If you ever have a slip-up with one of the fuel rods from a nuclear plant, it would be bad news. It would be sucked up like a tornado way up into the atmosphere. Once that happens, it goes into the atmosphere and starts destroying planet after planet. Your pollution can escape into the atmosphere and eventually reach our planet and we're trying to stop that now," the Orions said.

"What can we do?"

"Every little bit helps. Red tape causes most of your problems. It takes so long to get something done to get through the red tape. There are too many chiefs and not enough Indians, and everyone is afraid to hurt someone's feelings or step over someone. You need to start taking charge."

The Orions continued to say they are sending us things to help with radiation. There is a blue jellyfish that they release every so often that absorb impurities from the ocean. They do their job sailing across the ocean, then wash ashore and die. We call them Velella Velella. After learning this, it made Sydney think about discoveries of new species and how scientists say they've found a new species, but they have no idea and to what extent. They don't know that those jellyfish were put on the planet by extraterrestrials and how many other species do something for the planet. Everything has a purpose.

Sydney was able to see these blue jellyfish with a fin when she traveled to the beach in 2014 to Cambria, California where there were hundreds of thousands of them. If you've ever heard of the Red Rain and remembered how people were scratching their heads over this phenomenon, the Orions sent it down to cleanse impurities in the air and vegetation.

"Why are we seeing an increase in UFO activity in California now?"

"It's because you are at a bad time there on Earth with your pollution. You don't care enough or do enough. New York is very polluted and they take their trash out to the ocean and dump it. Don't even put your toe in the Hudson as a lot of chemicals are dumped there."

The Orions shared so much new information that we as humans have never thought of before. Sydney often wondered why us? Why were we receiving information that no one on the planet has?

They gave other warnings that our water reserves are too low and we need to drudge lakes and make them deeper and build more lakes-deep lakes, and aqueducts and capture water from freeways and purify it. "You are in for a drought, and you are letting precious water from rain run into the ocean." They also said that cutting down mountains is one of the worse things we could be doing. It's causing vortexes and we will start getting tornados and sandstorms. It's going to change the weather in all these different places around the world. The mountains were put there for a reason, in that formation.

Beverly continued with her channeling of the Orions who had a lot to say, "Does anybody sit down and start thinking about diabetes? It's from stuff that gets in your food. Some people can't fight it off. It makes the pancreas real weak. A lot of your food contains harsh chemicals and preservatives that are not good. Preservatives are killing people. You're preserving your innards which are dying. They're getting hard, clogged, and having a hard time functioning. We think a lot of it is caused by ingredients that put a shelf life on things.

Quit being so fast, quit wanting things and wanting them too fast, and wanting the wrong things. Be happy with what you have. People have lost their artistic abilities. People should enjoy Earth. Instead of going to a bar, go to the mountains and paint a picture.

You need to go back in time. Everybody's putting money in everybody else's palms. They're all on the take and the quality of life is going down the drain. You're spoiled and no one wants to say no. We can't give up; we are trying to help as much as we can. You didn't have all these diseases before, why now? No wonder there are so many deformed children. Warts, tumors, cancers. Your system can't filter it all out. That's how cancer develops.

When they put all that stuff in the water it takes out all of the minerals you need. Then when they try to fix something, they make it worse. It's best to leave it as it was, but we understand why it's done. You're better off with well water. Minerals are important for your brain. Your doctors are wondering why people are getting Alzheimer's. What they put in the water is making their brain slow down, and then they get a wrench in it. Their brain is coated with chemicals. They don't want to admit it's their fault, the people putting chemicals in the water.

Autism is caused by plastic with petroleum and fluoride. It's still pollution no matter how you look at it. Autism is also caused by leaving the vaccine medicine out too long that they give children. The medicine goes bad, is injected into the child, and it goes directly to the brain and causes something like crystals on the brain.

When you made yourselves comfortable with the things you produced, you made it worse for the environment. You need to go back to how it was. China is one of the worst polluters. Every day each person needs to do something to make things better. Do with what they have since the more they want, the more they pollute. Everyone needs to clean up their own backyard. All the plastics coming from China and Japan are bad news.

Your government doesn't care. It's happening in front of everyone's face, and no one says anything. But we don't want to give up hope. We have been doing this for a long time. You are very complex people, and we didn't make you to be that way either. You need to be shook up. Your President needs to speak on the small things that are really big and get back to family. Enjoy the small things in this world because they're good things. Get back to values and respect for each other and the land.

We do send down beings that are almost human and are programmed through their mind. They don't have any feelings at all, and the reason is that they have a job to do. So when they poke you with a needle, they don't think about it hurting, then they bring specimens back to us. We have to check on you because your pollution is getting out of hand. We have tried for so many years because we saw this coming. It's not like we can see the future, it's only common sense. That two and two make four and four and four make eight and eight and eight make sixteen in that sort of speaking or thinking is how we can see."

"That's how they could see that this was coming on," Beverly said.

"When will you make yourselves known?" Asked Sydney.

"About forty years. You're not ready. We're trying to save you now. You're polluting everything. You are moving forward in the wrong way. When we look at a child, they are smarter than you in many ways. They have been there and done that and learned but you don't. It's like money and material things control your lives to where you cannot see, you cannot hear, you don't use your senses and you don't use them right."

Beverly chimed in, "They are really kind of fed up with us. They have been to every part of our world trying in different languages to teach and tell people about pollution. About things they should and shouldn't do and we are the hardest people to convince to do anything because we are all in denial or we turn our back and expect other people to take care of our problems. Everyone leaves it to the other guy."

The Orions continued, "People should read up on the old ways to stay safe, be warm, and not hurt the Earth. You are pickling yourselves and that's why your organs aren't functioning well. One organ is the brain. The thyroid is the living source of the body. It controls your brain and body functions. The big mushrooms, the portabella ones help with removing toxins from the body."

"They're saying mistakes were made in making us. We don't do anything about problems until it's too late. We were here to enjoy life, but we're destroying it. The government doesn't care. It's happening in front of everyone's face, and no one says anything. Many people are helping with the destruction of mankind. They don't want to give up hope. They have been doing this for a long time," Beverly said.

"You don't hear and you don't see. You ignore what we try to tell and show you. You were our hope, but you are

demolishing the hope. You are polluting everything. You are very complex people and we didn't make you to be that way either, but we feel responsible because we are the ones who put you together."

The Orions explained how they know everything that is happening on our planet. They have people on the planet they send to keep an eye on things. Some of the people they put on the planet get into government positions to expose bad people to get them thrown out. They also said that a lot of people who go missing, or die are these people. The people end up going home to their planet after they've completed their mission.

And for everyone to get on the same page, they need to all express their dislikes and stick with them. Our courage for standing up for ourselves, we've almost lost it. You pay for a planet to live on and you shouldn't have to. Our electric utility is being so monopolized that the small man has no chance to even stick up for himself or his beliefs and feelings. They are trying to take away people's way of life at their own expense. They said life is a never-ending battle, it's like taking dominos and stacking them in a circle, it never goes anywhere, and it just comes back to where it was. You can't just touch the leaf of the flower; you have to touch the whole flower.

The Orions continued, "The people who get the awards, such as the Nobel Peace Prize, those are the people we like to associate with. They're trying to make a better Earth. They were crucified for thinking the way they think, more or less. Nelson Mandela and Martin Luther King Jr were good men. They weren't liked because they were too likable and too honest. Martin Luther King Jr. was doing too much good for Black people and leniency. That's why he was killed."

"There are a lot of cures that are so simple, but you don't want cures because it's all about money and cancer is big business. A lot of physicians and pharmacists are afraid to be honest, they're afraid of their peers."

"You can buy anything on Earth, even death."

After this, Sydney went outside by herself where she was far away from the house. She went to ask for guidance and the wisdom to go about the environmental issues. After, she went back into the house and sat at the kitchen table. Her mother's back was to her as she was playing a game on her computer which sat against a wall. Before Sydney got settled into her seat, Beverly turned around and began to explain how to go about it. Stunned, Sydney grabbed her pen and paper and took down what they said. She was thinking to herself, "Do they hear my prayers? They must have because when I said it, I was outside saying it in my mind."

The Orions spoke, "Plan it out, what you're going to say. Choose who will be there. List all the things that have happened in this world. Every word has to count." This reading of Sydney's mind would happen several more times to the point she knew they were reading it regularly. She realized it was part of their communication.

Sydney looked at her mother and thanked the Orions for their time and help. And then the Orions said one last thing, ***"We would like for you to do more to help the homeless."***

Sydney knew what the Orions said is the truth. We keep leaving the pollution for the next guy to fix and because we reincarnate, we are the next guy.

Because we're coming back.

CHAPTER 6

Programmed Prototypes

The Orions provided information about the grey beings they created as their workers. Other advanced races also made greys as helpers. They are programmed and therefore do not have a soul. The Orions are quoted below:

"When we made the greys, we wanted them to look very different. This way when you saw one, you knew it came from another world."

"We call the greys by the job they do. We call them Seekers and Retrievers."

"The greys are a combination of biological material and mechanical apparatus."

"They have a chip at the back of their head. We shoot it into there with air."

"We call the Mantis beings Carriers. They have long arms and can carry a lot of things. Everything has a purpose. There is a purpose for short greys and tall greys. What one can't do, the other can."

There are Seekers, Retrievers, and Senders. "They have a chip in their brain that instructs them, and it doesn't stray left, and it doesn't stray right. It's exact." They are programmed to do a job and nothing more. These beings think in a straight line, meaning they don't go outside of their programming.

The grey beings have cameras in their eyes, and a dark lens covers them. They take pictures and send them back to Orion. The Orions can see through the eyes of the greys and can see through the eyes of humans as well. Although they do it rarely, they do this with Sydney and her mother. The greys absorb food through their skin and can only speak telepathically. There can be bad ones, and good ones. It's all in how they're programmed. They could program humans as well if they wanted to.

"You were going to serve us like the greys, but something in the DNA changed. The DNA came from different planets and there was something in the DNA that completely went off track. We knew it right away, but there was nothing we could do about it. It would have been destroying something alive."

They created a programmed human-sized praying mantis being by taking the DNA from a small praying mantis insect. The mantis beings are called Carriers because they have long arms to reach high places and carry medical supplies to the spaceships. They go with the Seekers on the ships. The mantis beings are kept in a pen on their planet in the Orion constellation. They are happy and know a no different way of life.

The stories about greys making hybrids with humans seem to have presented different reasons. The people of Orion explained to Sydney that the grey beings are making hybrids with humans because they are trying to make a better being. The reason for that, is because the greys have very thin skin, and they get too hot or cold. That is why they don't like coming to Earth when it's too hot or cold. Why the Orions don't fix this issue with them, Sydney does not know. They do seem to have autonomy from the Orions.

Sydney learned the reason for some abductions is because they're making a better human. The advanced races are taking from humans and crossing the DNA with an advanced person. That is why there are these advanced children you hear about, the ones graduating college as a child. They are put back on Earth with foster families who usually know who they are, and these children are to become doctors and scientists. They will make the world better, and their bodies can handle pollution better.

The greys come to Earth and check on humans, all humans regardless of which advanced race they belong to. They collect samples of hair, blood, skin, and bodily fluids to take back to Orion to be tested, to see how humans are doing in their environment. They are looking for the effects of pollution on the human body. The greys also come to Earth to fix problems with humans and are also here to learn medical procedures. And the reason for people healed after an encounter with grey beings. They do have medical facilities in the ocean.

"The greys are a combination of biological material and mechanical apparatus."

Sydney was at a UFO conference when a woman she met wondered why she was picked up multiple times. She didn't mind, but she just wanted to know. Sydney called her mother and asked her about this woman. Beverly said she was picked up to fix a defect she had. Sydney put her mother on speaker so the woman could hear, and Beverly explained the greys had given her a thick protein lining in her stomach because her system didn't absorb nutrients right. The Orions explained that this made the greys "One-up in their skills and they are saving her life." The woman was blown away by the conversation since she felt something was wrong with her stomach. Sydney found it amazing that the Orions can answer questions about a specific person and know them.

There are things the Orions told Sydney that made her and the people around her rethink everything they knew. For instance, when you're asleep and your body jerks awake because you feel like you're falling? They said that a grey is doing that. Aside from picking people up and taking samples, they can hover at your bedroom window and pick up your body telepathically, flip it over and check you out. If they set you down abruptly, that's when you feel like you're falling, and jerk awake. Later, Sydney saw a blog on the internet where a woman woke up while being levitated from her bed, then was put down and it made her instantly think of the greys.

A few days before this was told to Sydney, it happened to her. The next day after that, it happened again. It was like they wanted to prove to Sydney it was real. They said everyone has come in contact with a grey, they have just been unaware of it.

"When we made the greys, we wanted them to look very different. This way when you saw one you knew it came from another world."

Learning about reptilians was a bit of a mystery and the Orions lent some information on them but were not able to say who created them. Reptilians are not programmed, and they do have a soul, which surprised Sydney. Reptilians also make hybrids with humans by mating with them and they do this by disguising themselves to look different and appealing. It's believed they do this by putting an image in someone's mind. All people on Earth are hybrids from the advanced people that made them. And yes, some people have reptilian DNA, but this is not always a bad thing. But it did make Sydney think of all of the bad people that have come to her.

This new information about reptilians having a soul really made Sydney think. She had asked the Orions about animals and if they had a soul, to which they replied, "Animals do not have a soul; they are programmed, in a way. They are programmed with instincts." When you think about it, it must be the same way for humans as well. We have instincts to survive and reproduce.

The Orions explained the bad ones can't be trusted, and the good ones are trying to be more human. They don't want to be reptilians; they have a thing fighting in their brain that tells them they're bad or good. The good tells them they want to be more human. They don't like how their people are, so they try to look more human by growing human skin. They also take human DNA and put it in theirs. What they do is take skin cells from fresh human bodies that just died. They scratch the cells off and they grow skin by putting them in containers that have a chemical in them. The lumpy skin is then grown in a tube and stretched out and laid on a bumpy surface. They have to lance their fingers and remove their skin and the new skin grows over it.

When they told this to Sydney's mother, they flashed a picture in her mind of a device that holds back the skin on an arm so that the new skin can be laid into the area. The device pushes their skin away while the other skin grows. The DNA they collected from humans, is put in their body so it's more accepting of it. After a while, they can just stretch it over their own skin and the DNA from it will grow into theirs. Little by little they take pieces. They need to get some of our blood too. They try to look more human but the problem they're having is with their eyes, ears, tongue, and feet. A lot of beings from other planets are doing that.

"Some reptilians have a spark of good in them because they started out with a little of our DNA. That DNA did something to their brain that sparked them into a knowing and wanting of something different than what they do and who they are," the Orions explained.

The bad reptilians are afraid. They can be likened to people on Earth who like to spread rumors and cause chaos. Sometimes these people are a lower class in their thinking because they are not elevated in their minds to behave respectfully, with morals. Well, the bad reptilians are like that. They are the lower class of the advanced races. They are afraid of being found out and do everything they can to scare people. They are afraid for themselves and their future, so they try to gain control. But who created them? Remember, God created everything.

In all, these reptilians are nothing to fear, because the most evil species is the human.

CHAPTER 7

Negative Forces

As an extreme empath who feels everything, it was hard to know how to deal with the horrible people who came into Sydneys life. People would often flock to her and treat her terribly for no reason. She was constantly questioning herself, why did she feel so strongly? Why did she dislike people? Why did others pain pierce her heart? It wasn't until her awakening that she came to understand it.

Since she was a little girl, evil was always knocking at her door. So many of the people that came into her life were bipolar, narcissists, and sociopaths. One person even poisoned her. Then there were people who came to her and confessed things just out of the blue. She always seemed to be the person that people came to for comfort. But in the back of her mind, she always had this feeling there was going to be a great evil she would have to face.

During this wake-up, she had a dream that she was standing in a mall. In the dream, she was looking down from above at herself.

A person approached her and said, "They're coming." Sydney became nervous and didn't know what to do. Just then, a rush of people came at her, pulling and tearing at her clothes. Something came over Sydney saying that if she showed them love, it would change. She tried her best to do so, and the people started going all around her. All the people that came into her life wanted her help. The dream interaction was a learning tool for how to cope with people. She felt she was receiving help through these dreams.

There were times that she would see young children while she was out. She would say nothing to them, and they would always smile or come talk to her. One of those times she was behind a mother holding a baby in line at a store. The baby looked over his mother's shoulder, smiled big and tried several times to jump from his mother's arms to hers. She often wondered if they knew her somehow on a soul level or perhaps, they were another bad soul looking for help.

On another occasion, Sydney had some renters on her property. They came home while she was sitting outside, near where they usually park. She didn't normally interact with them too much to give them privacy, but they had two little girls and the strangest thing happened. The man pulled up with his girls in the back after a day at the lake and one child, Charlie who was half asleep, got out of the car and sprinted to Sydney. She ran up to and gave Sydney the longest hug without stopping. She was confused because she thought Charlie was mistaking Sydney for her mother, who was in her unit. Perhaps she was half asleep, but that wasn't the case at all. She would not let go of Sydney. It was the sweetest thing, then her dad had to finally come pull her off. Sydney felt these children know her and can be good souls or bad souls.

But the bad people that have come to Sydney want her to forgive them. They keep coming back each lifetime with an issue because they did something bad in their previous life and never broke that cycle. And then they reincarnated with a mental issue. They want her to help them escape that by forgiving their sins…. or could there be something else more sinister happening?

During her awakening, the bad people in Sydney's life increased. They never stopped coming, one after another. She was driving home from work and while nearing a bridge, a person jumped off it into the lane next to her. It was odd because the traffic wasn't particularly light that day, yet cars were going slow enough to miss hitting the body. Sydney saw the body in the air after the man had jumped from the other side of the bridge. She saw his body land on his side with his one arm extended and his head landed on it. His body bounced about four inches. Sydney's car was one of the nearest to the body and she didn't know what to do except slow down and continue so as not to cause an accident. Once she was up ahead, she pulled over to take in what had just happened. She was very sad for the person that his life was so bad this was his only way out of pain. She was sad for a few days and even cried, but the thought crossed her mind that perhaps this was another person looking for her help. It was also being reported that within two weeks, there were two more bridge jumpers on the same freeway Sydney traveled each day. Something strange was happening.

The more Sydney got the word out about the Orions, the negative entities coming to her in her dreams increased and became more intense and scarier. She was being swayed from telling her story. There were several times while she slept, she was held down in her bed with her mouth covered. She would try to yell in her sleep while trying to move. Another time she was held down with her nose and mouth closed. It was the first time it went that far. Once she was finally freed from it, she sat up in her bed and gasped for air.

Sydney reflected when she once worked for a store as a teenager how a man started berating her and saying awful things to her. There was no reason for it and he made her cry. He was just an awful man who seemed to get pleasure from hurting others. Many years later during her awakening period, Sydney was leaving her friend's house, about to get on the freeway. A woman who was going opposite of her, turned left right in front of her. She had to slam on her brakes to avoid hitting her. Moments later, Sydney was sitting at a light next to a woman on her left. Sydney's lane took her to the ramp to get on the freeway. The woman's lane was intended to make a left turn. The light turned green and the woman quickly proceeded to move on over into Sydney's lane, cutting her off. She had to swerve and put on her brakes to avoid hitting the woman. She finally got on the freeway when moments later, a guy sped up and got in front of her, cutting her off and slowing down so that he could get over to the right lane to get to the exit on the right. Again, she had to slam on her brakes to avoid hitting him. He turned and looked back at her like she was the problem, shrugging his shoulders.

Shaken, Sydney had to pull off the freeway and compose herself. It was then Sydney saw a text from her friend that she had been visiting who said she left her alien drawings at her house. When Sydney reflected back on these things and many other instances, she began to feel these occurrences were created by the negative forces who tormented her all of her life.

On a separate occasion, a reptilian entity showed her a video in her mind of her laying on her stomach; on a wood floor in an empty room with only one door to get out. Everything was wood, wood floor, wood walls and door. They slid her body toward the door and all she could think about was getting out that door. They slid her body back from the door and then toward the door several times, trying to torment and scare her.

Finally it stopped, and she woke up. She had even experienced being held down about a year before her awakening but had no idea what to think about it at that time. Again, she was trying to yell for help and could not move.

Another night Sydney was startled awake by something that got in her face and yelled. It wasn't a person; it was a reptilian face. It got right into her face in her mind's eye and roared loudly until she immediately sat up out of deep sleep. She felt that it was trying to deter her from what she was doing, what she was learning.

The scary experiences continued when Sydney arrived home one day from work. It was the same day her roommate left for a couple of weeks. As soon as she stepped inside the door, she immediately felt an intense energy. It was suffocating to where she could not breathe. She was very nervous and shaking. She thought about leaving, but she had nowhere to go. She called her mother. "Mom, I just got home and there is some presence in the house. I feel it strongly." "They said it is a spirit looking for your roommate," her mother said. Sydney did not believe this as she felt it was a reptilian presence. She decided to be brave and inspect the entire house, going to the garage and to each bedroom upstairs and looking in closets. Eventually it went away, but Sydney felt the reptilians were there, tormenting her with their presence. That same night Sydney had a dream of a large reptilian male in her bedroom spreading mold all over her walls while she laid in her bed coughing. The vision in her mind changed to showing reptilians jumping into bodies of several people who were the bad people that came into her life who treated her terribly. Were they being controlled by the reptilians or did they have reptilian DNA?

She learned to start asking for protection from these entities from her Guardian Angel. Once before she went to bed after asking for protection, she woke up to being held down with her mouth covered again but this time only for a second. It was like something stepped in and smacked it away. A few weeks later; the same thing repeated. Her prayers and asking for help were working.

Later on, Sydney's mother told her that these entities can't hurt her. They're just trying to deter her from telling their story because they don't want it to get out, because the reptilians fear for themselves. Since her awakening Beverly, too had multiple experiences of being held down in her bed.

The Orions went on to inform her mother that another alien race tried to pick her up, but the Orions stopped them. Beverly felt it was a reptilian race that tried to pick her up to stop her from having Sydney because Sydney was the single most important person that attracted bad people and reptilians. She was the main target, and that was the evil she battled since birth.

CHAPTER 8

Flashbacks

In the middle of the awakening of Sydney and Beverly, Sydney reflected back on the strange occurrences in their lives that brought them to this moment of discovery. She had a moment of looking back on her life growing up and the interesting things her mother told her. They were all connected to what she was to realize later in life. Sydney's awakening caused many flashbacks of the odd feelings, thoughts, and occurrences.

It all made sense why she felt so different and struggled to fit in. From the time she was very young she was thinking and doing things that she didn't understand. She thought about the time she was around three years old, and her mother was pregnant. She was standing next to her mother in the living room when a thought entered her mind saying, *"If I was born from my mother, then how was the first person made?"* This thought made her immediately look at her mother with her large belly and baby growing inside. This was an odd thing for a three-year-old to be thinking since she didn't fully understand what it meant at that age.

She was an odd child who did odd things. When she was five, she lived behind a Baptist Church and would hear singing every Sunday. The home they lived in was owned by the church. She was a very curious child, so one Sunday morning she got up, put on a dress, and went to the church where she listened to the pastor for all of two minutes. She was the only child in the Church and received a lot of strange looks from the adults. But she didn't care, for a quiet, shy child, she could be rather bold. For some reason, she just had an urge to find out about the church. Since she did not understand what was being preached, she soon returned home to her mother who was still sleeping. For some silly reason, she repeated the same thing the next weekend.

Sydney came from a large family and from very early on felt different. She could see evil all around her. She sat back and studied people, most always predicting what a person was going to do next. The other girls would always tease her for being different. It's something that never changed in all her years. People were always cruel, and evil flocked to her.

Growing up, she became fascinated with war movies and that would never change. She wondered about the wars, the hate, the greed. How can someone kill another person? She couldn't fathom this. Since her awakening, she became aware that she was to learn all about people and was part of understanding humans.

When Sydney was about five-years-old, in the late sixties, her father took her to buy a Halloween costume. She was so excited because she knew which costume she wanted. This was so special because out of five children, he was spending time with just her. They went to the nearby mall that had a drug store located within it and found their way to the back of the store where the costumes were. Her father kneeled next to her, looking at her with love and a smile, as she looked over the costumes. Before she got to the store she knew exactly what she wanted, but now found herself confused over two. In the square box with the see-through plastic covering, there was the princess costume and then there was the witch costume. She made her choice, but it wasn't what she initially wanted. She went in wanting to be a scary witch but came out with the princess costume instead. She chose good over evil.

About a year later, when she was six years old, she was standing in her mother's bedroom and had a moment of reflection about being, just being. She looked at her arms, her hands, then twirled around to see behind herself. She felt like she was in a dense body, trying to grasp being in a physical body. It seemed like wherever she came from before, maybe her body wasn't this dense. Sydney couldn't figure out what these thoughts meant, so she thought maybe she was just being silly.

Not long after, Sydney was outside playing hopscotch next to a couple older ladies she didn't know, while her mother was off in the distance. While playing hopscotch, her eyes met the older women who told her, "You are going to do something very special." Sydney just looked at them and gave a little smile. She continued playing hopscotch without saying anything back.

Growing up she had a normal childhood except for the extreme shyness and sometimes odd thoughts. And then there were the terrible people. It seemed things were placed in her path so that she would know her awakening was real and that what she was about to learn was real. When she started first grade at a new school, the teacher asked the class who would like to show her around the school and one girl put her hand up right away. Her name was Sharon. Sydney would not realize for decades just how important a role Sharon was to play in her life. It was almost like the very outgoing Sharon was there to pull Sydney out of her shyness. And she did. When Sharon and Sydney walked home together that day, they realized they lived right behind one another. What an odd coincidence. They became best friends and remained friends throughout their lives.

A couple years later they shared another class in third grade. And the teacher said something to the class which was strange. She didn't understand why the teacher brought it up and to third graders no less, but her teacher said that one time a man put his thoughts into her head. She said it scared her and she told him to never do that again. At the time Sydney remembered saying to herself, "How can someone put their thoughts into someone else's head?" Sydney called these odd things cherry bombs that were put in her path for when she awakened later in life.

For the next few years Sydney and Sharon were together all the time as best pals. They would spend their birthdays, holidays, and sometimes vacations together. They would walk home from school together every day. Sometimes they would go a different way, passing a church. Every time they walked by the church, Sydney's fascination reappeared. She wanted to know what it was all about, just like when she was five and snuck into the church behind her house. What went on in that church? What was it all about and why did Sydney need to know?

Sharon went on to get Sydney involved in sports. They played on basketball teams and softball teams, and they made more friends together. She was exactly what Sydney needed. It's like this was set up because she needed to have someone nudge her, to pull her out of her shyness for what she was to do later in her life.

When Sydney was nine-years-old, something unfortunate was about to happen. Sydney had a bad feeling, and the next time she saw her father she wanted to be sure he knew that she loved him. She was so quiet and shy, even with him. By this time her parents had been separated and he was living elsewhere.

So the next time she saw him she ran to him and jumped into his arms. A week later, he died. Later as an adult, when she was told Orions took people sometimes, she wondered if they took him as part of her awakening process. An idea that would be hard to digest.

After being out of school for a week due to her father's death, she eventually had to return to class. She was still in a state of shock, finding herself staring at the walls. Her teacher noticed this and went to talk to her. Mrs. Rathburn told her how both of her parents died in a car crash. As Sydney was looking up at her, her eyes were beginning to tear up. But that shy person in her held them back from streaming down her face. She couldn't have someone see her cry. She blinked and they disappeared. Mrs. Rathburn asked her if she wanted to go home, and Sydney said no. She knew it was time for her to get back to normal life, and she had to be strong. She was very grown-up for a young girl. Mrs. Rathburn then offered her a ticket to a movie that was playing in the cafeteria after school. It was that act of kindness from her teacher that snapped her out of it. Sydney said there need to be more people in the world like Mrs. Rathburn.

The interest in God, the Bible, and the church reappeared when she went to the Swap Meet with her mom. She never asked for anything when she went shopping with her mom, that's just how she was. She figured she didn't need anything important enough to take away from her family. Walking through the aisles, she came upon a necklace with a red cross on it. It was her first time asking for something, and she felt she had to have it. Her mother bought it for her as her first cross necklace. It's all she wanted.

After getting her necklace, Sydney started reading the Bible every night and something odd happened. She was lying on her bunk bed and a strange thought came into her head saying, "The

Bible is the word of man and not God." She was still too young and naïve to understand that an odd thought like that couldn't have come from herself. Why would she think that? She took the thought in a negative way and stopped reading the Bible. Sydney didn't have anything against the Bible as an adult, she understood then that whoever put the thought in her mind just wanted her to know it was written by man, and that's okay. God wrote the Ten Commandments. Later in life, she would pick up the Bible again and have a better understanding. She was too young at the time to even understand what she was reading anyway. Looking back, she felt strongly that she was to learn about God and the story of Jesus so she could be reminded of why she was here.

One day after school, Sydney was with Sharon when another girl started a fight with Sydney. She went to punch Sydney in the arm and to her surprise, she missed. She watched the punch, almost like it was in slow motion, heading for her right shoulder. She saw it come at her as she watched her fist go beyond her arm. Sydney's thoughts of her missing her arm were quickly cut short when she saw that she was still coming at her. She proceeded to put her head down and punch Sydney in the abdomen repeatedly. Sydney was not a fighter, so she didn't do anything. She just froze. What happened was wild; her punches never made contact with Sydney. She stood there and watched her fists come close to her abdomen. Several times they came within an inch, but no contact. She then let up and walked away, almost robotic, not even questioning why her own fists didn't touch. Sydney couldn't understand what happened.

As Sydney got older, there were many occasions she caught herself staring out into space as if she was thinking. A few times people would catch her doing this and ask her, "Where are you?" Which would quickly bring her back to reality. Over the years she realized this was a way she would meditate, although she didn't realize she was doing it. It was the way she figured things out, the way she got answers. Things came to her in this state.

There were a couple of occasions with the most recent occurrence right before her awakening, that Sydney would find herself just standing with a grin on her face, like a cat who got the canary. She knew she had a secret. Something would come to her and then she would get excited and giggle. But the thing is, consciously she didn't know what that secret was or why she would giggle for no reason; she just knew she had a secret that was great and that no one knew about. Even at the time, she was questioning what this meant.

Sydney would grow up wondering about how life got to this planet and if there was a God. She was questioning everything. Several times she would look out at the sky say to herself, "I want to know," but those thoughts began to take a back seat when she married and had children. Her focus for many years was on raising children and not much else. It was when the children were out of the home that her awakening began. She had some communication, but she didn't realize it was communication with the Orions. All of that would come to light upon her awakening.

Her life was hard because of the energies she felt. She didn't have a very happy life, but tried as best she could to smile and not think of how much she didn't want to be on Earth. She was on the outside looking in and was always worried about something. She could never enjoy herself because she didn't feel right in her own skin. Sydney was a magnet for bad people.

Her awakening process began slowly when she went to a department store and saw a necklace in the window that she just had to have. When she saw the cross on the necklace, it took her back to the memory of when she bought her first cross with her mom at the swap meet. It triggered those thoughts again about

God and how the world was populated. Sydney rarely bought jewelry, especially anything expensive, but for some reason, she had to have this necklace. She walked away at first, but came back eventually to buy it. She then began having experiences of being held down with her mouth covered, trying to yell and scream. In real life she was making all kinds of noise with her mouth closed, struggling to wake up out of a nightmare. Little did she realize this was the start of her awakening. The negative forces knew and were trying to stop her.

Both Sydney and her mother were very down-to-earth, hard-working people with a great sense of humor. They enjoyed the simple things in life, like hiking, taking a walk, or talking to people and learning about their families. Sydney said her mother was the most positive person she knew. She could take a potentially bad situation and turn it around without even trying. It's like she had the kill-them-with-kindness thing down, but that was just her and not an act.

Her mother grew up in the forties and fifties and had a magnetic personality. Everyone loved Beverly and she was so much fun to be with. Even she had experiences in her life it seemed that she was supposed to experience, things she was directed to. When she was a teenager, she was sent to live in a convent by her parents, because her father worked away from their home and her mother was very sick and could not care for her. In the convent, she was known as Kathleena Philomena Marie Shepherd and she was there for two and a half years.

During her time at the convent, Beverly saw to it that it would not be a boring place. She kept it hopping and there was never a dull moment while she was there. Beverly found herself sent to the corner many times for getting into trouble. She explained a time when she was the softball catcher and Sister Philomena was up to bat when a gust of air blew her habit forward to reveal a shiny bald head. Beverly had no idea they were bald and could not contain her laughter. She ended up falling backward on the ground laughing so hard. She went to the corner for a week.

On another occasion at dinner, Beverly saw bugs in the macaroni. She told her friend Daisy to tell the next girl to her right, and Beverly did the same on the left until all two-hundred-and-fifty girls got the message. Somehow Mother Germain was able to determine who started the rumor and called Kathleena Philomena to the front and asked her, "Why did you tell everyone there are bugs in the macaroni, don't you realize that's more protein?" Mother Germain then slapped Beverly on the butt and told her to go back to her table.

Mother Charles was very stern and never smiled. Beverly wanted to break that in her, so one day she hid in the closet where the cleaning supplies were. When Mother Charles opened the door, Beverly lunged and growled until Mother Charles fell backward, caught totally off guard. Beverly went to the corner for a week.

When Beverly wasn't getting into trouble and had some time for herself, she would go sit in a window seat and sing Ave Maria. She loved the song and it echoed throughout the church.

When it was time for her to leave the convent, she went around to the sisters and said her goodbyes. But she didn't know where Mother Germain was and asked Sister Philomena. Sister Philomena told her that she wasn't supposed to say anything, but Mother Germain was in her room crying and she was too upset to come say goodbye. She said, "Mother Germain has never cried over anybody before, but she's crying over you." And this is how Beverly affects people and nothing has changed to this day.

And then there was the incident in 1958 when she and her cousin saw the spaceship a couple of years later.

As she moved on throughout her life, Beverly probably should have died four times, it seemed someone must have been watching

CHAPTER 9

Experiences

One night Sydney went to bed not feeling well with a lot of pain. In the middle of the night, she experienced seeing a dark shadow over her eyes. Her eyes were closed, but she could see a darkness that seemed to move from her head down to her feet. She was held down like she had been in the past. The next day she called her mother to tell her about it, and the Orions told her that Sydney, in desperation, reached out through another dimension and caught the attention of an entity going by as if to be asking for help. It was a good entity and it needed to hold Sydney down so that it could x-ray her body and that was reason for the darkness. They told her that she did that herself, she broke through to another dimension.

The experiences didn't stop there. She met people in various spiritual communities who directed her through this awakening that she felt she was having. She had received readings from several different gifted people who would all inform her of the same information, that she was special.

The crazy awakening experiences went off like fireworks for the first few months, then became sparse. It had been months since Sydney had a dream that she knew was not a regular dream. She dreamt that she was holding a man's gold ring. It looked just like the ring from *Lord of the Rings*. It looked big, but when she put it on it took shape around her finger and fit perfectly. She wondered what this meant. A couple days later upon awaking, she received a message that said, *"I hold the key."*

She knew her friend Mark was put in her path to show her around to legitimate gifted people in the community. He directed her to the right people, and she had the most amazing readings and experiences. It seemed that all the things she was going through were to make her understand and realize what she was to later find out. She kept getting reading after reading that kept pointing to the same thing. She gave no information because she wanted to be sure the readings were true and real.

Mark brought Sydney to a psychic fair and decided to try a reading there. She came upon a woman named Debbie who specialized in speaking to loved ones who have passed on. Something was so strong in her that she had to do this. People there were trying to suggest she see another person, but something told her to see Debbie. She wanted to face the one thing that haunted her all of her life. It was her father who had passed away when she was nine. She had anxiety and a deep hurt from losing him early. The last time she saw him, he was in a casket, and was nervous about touching him, but she managed to put her picture in his hand with the encouragement of a family friend.

She found herself across from Debbie and had noticed the tissue box under the seat before sitting down. Debbie asked who she wanted to call upon and Sydney said she wanted to speak to her father. She said he was there but there was also a female that came forward. Giving her no information, Debbie went on to say that he was proud of her, that she did a good job and that she should be proud. He said he had regrets about how he lived his life and that he is working on that with God now. He said that Sydney can be quiet and just take things and then finally will just blow up and tell people off. Sydney laughed because it was so true. Then he said the latter part is from him. Again she laughed. He also said not to feel remorse for past relationships and that he was happy that she has learned how to pinpoint the issues so as not to repeat certain things in the future. There was much more that was said but it was too personal. Sydney cried and cried the rest of the evening, but she felt so much better. She kept thinking of the other ways Debbie could have known such details about her and her father but concluded that she must be talking to him. Sydney's father asked her to tell her brothers and sisters that he loved them and so she called her brother and told him. She couldn't stop crying.

Sydney didn't know what to make of all of the readings she was getting from all of these gifted people:

"You are so important," Aaron said.

"You put your mother on a pedestal, but you are more powerful," Debra said.

"They're telling me you're special. You are very special," Maham said.

She tried to figure out what all of the strange occurrences and thoughts meant. She couldn't put her thumb on what was happening and she was confused.

Sydney was finally able to get her mother to attend a UFO conference, which she just loved. She loved being amongst other people just like her. They all did a lot of walking around and looking at crystals together. The Orions would comment on the best ones to buy. They attended a speaker session, then walked around the speakers' tables. Sydney introduced her mother to Travis Walton who was sitting at a table selling his book. Immediately she was getting downloads from the Orions on him about his abduction experience. They told her mother that Travis was very affected by the abduction. Then they offered a piece of information that no one had. They told her that Travis Walton interrupted the greys who were picking up animals and doing testing on them. The greys picked up this being they didn't expect, which was Travis. The Orions explained that those greys were programmed to only pick up animals, so when they got a human, they treated him rough, like they did with the animals. It was no wonder Travis was terrified.

Sydney decided to join a class to help further her own psychic abilities. During one particular session, she was partnered with a woman. This was done through the phone, so they couldn't see each other. It was called a Rose Ceremony, and they were to give each other a reading that involved two roses. Sometimes this ability kicked in for Sydney and other times, she got nothing. This time it worked and Sydney was able to give the woman a reading. She asked about herself, and about a friend of hers who she was thinking about. Sydney told her she saw the two roses wrap around each other. "You are connected, intertwined. You are very different people, but the same," Sydney said. "Yes, that's very true," the woman responded. It was then time for Sydney to receive her reading. She asked about herself and her mother, giving her no extra information. The woman said she saw the two roses move and then form into a cross. Sydney's jaw dropped. She couldn't believe this vision was right. She and her mother are connected with the divine.

A spiritual church got Sydney's attention that she attended a few times. The pastor and two others always gave a healing at the end. Sydney had been dealing with illness for quite a while, so she decided to go up to the front and receive healing. The pastor of the church named Grace was the one who gave the healing. Sydney sat in a chair while Grace quietly did the healing. When she was done, she bent down and whispered, "During the healing, I saw all of these angels dressed in white with hands in the prayer position, lined up in the aisle. They said to me, thank you for healing her and they said they were from Orion." Shivers came over Sydney after hearing this. What was the reason for these important and miraculous interactions? She didn't know.

Mark sent Sydney to another healer. She really didn't want to go, but he persuaded her to. Carol was the healer, and she showed Sydney to a secluded room away from her house. Sydney laid on what looked like a comfortable massage table and put headphones on to listen to soothing music. Carol explained that she would be clearing Sydney's chakras which will aid in her recovery. The more she turned up the volume, the more she became detached, slipping into a deeply relaxed state. Carol told her to imagine herself free from worry. Sydney was completely relaxed. She let herself go.

When they finished, Carol explained that something happened that she's never experienced before. When she got to Sydney's second chakra, she said all of these spirits lined the top of the walls in the room, as if to be sitting on a shelf. Then she saw an image of water flowing over edges in all directions, like in a rectangle, and then Sydney's body emerged from the middle lying down with her arms spread out to the side and her head tilted back. As she went on, a flash of light entered the room they were in.

When she got to Sydney's third chakra, there were many blocks. It was row after row of black curtains. She got on one side of the curtain and a male spirit appeared on the other side. One by one they removed all of the curtains until they were gone. She said Sydney kept coming out of her body and she had to keep trying to get her back down. Sydney told her she didn't want to be in that body anymore. Those words made complete sense. Sydney went to her car and wrote down every detail of what Carol said, then went home. Sydney was thinking to herself, there are some really odd things going on, what does all of this mean?

The next time Sydney saw her mother, she told her about the spirits lining the top of the walls. The Orions chimed in and said those spirits came to help because Sydney is genuine. This was still early on in her awakening and she was experiencing a lot of these types of readings, visions, telepathic communications, and dream interactions.

It was also around this time that she knew she was being upgraded. She had trouble sleeping and could never sleep during the day, but she laid on the couch and went to sleep for several hours unable to get up. She felt pressure on her head which she had also experienced in the past. She could barely move, then she would go back to sleep.

Sydney was learning that if you ask for something before you go to bed, you may get an answer. So one night before Sydney went to bed, she asked the people out there, the guides or whoever was out there listening, what her name is "out there". She knew she was someone out there, she felt it. Interestingly enough, a name did come to her in the wee hours of the morning. She had put a pen and paper next to her before going to bed and upon waking she read the name "Indiose." She vaguely remembered writing it down, thinking it was a dream. But when she awoke the next morning, she saw it next to her and thought how strange, "That is my name when I am not in this body."

About a week later, Sydney went to go see a movie with one of her friends. She started walking up to the movie theater while her friend was lagging behind, getting something from the car. She was about to pass an older gentleman, about eighty years old, standing on the corner to the right of her. Out of the blue, he asked her, "What movie are you going to see?" She kind of fumbled the name of the movie saying, "Is heaven real, heaven is for real?" He just smiled at Sydney with this warm smile and then walked away to the parking lot. She wondered why he was standing there in the first place. She told her friend who thought it was strange too. Sydney felt strongly he was someone special and she knew who, the feeling was intense. She knew who he was but was having trouble believing it, and she was in shock. He needed to put himself there to make things real, and by this time he knew Sydney was paying attention. The man was God

CHAPTER 10

The Communication

S ydney received communications all throughout her life. A lot of it she didn't realize was extra-terrestrial contact and communication. Because she had no obvious contact or awareness of any such phenomena, she couldn't relate these thoughts to anything but her own, even though they were odd.

When she had the communication when she was three years old, and then again when she was nine years old, it seemed like her own thought. But the way to know it wasn't her thought was to realize whether it was normal to be thinking.

Sydney was lying in bed and was very upset about something going on in her life. She struggled to sleep and was tossing and turning when a voice came into her mind that said, "Don't worry, everything is going to be okay." She immediately sat up in bed and she knew this was real. She knew this came from the spirit world, and it was the first time she had this realization. The same thing repeated two weeks later when she again struggled to sleep due to being stressed. This time she told her family. She thought maybe it was her grandparents trying to comfort her.

Upon her awakening, the communication really took off. She believed this happened so that she could explain to people what these communications were like, and what her mother was experiencing. She had to experience it herself to be able to explain it.

It was found that Beverly has a very special gift. She has communication like no other. Sydney had done a lot of research and never found any gifted person that has telepathic communication with actual physical people on another planet. It was also found that Beverly can communicate with the dead and have two-way communication with them. Sydney and her mother had said they don't blame anyone for not believing. They wouldn't believe it either.

A few months into her awakening, Sydney was at a restaurant bar with a friend celebrating her birthday. She had a couple of drinks and was having a great time. She was so relaxed and happy but then suddenly felt immense pressure on the top of her head. A message was coming through and she quickly went outside to where her friend was. She kept saying, "Whoa, whoa" and her friend knew exactly what was happening. "Write it down, write it down," her friend said. So Sydney sat down on the curb and typed out the message she received.

"The difference looking from my world to this world. Looking at it at another angle. Knowledge I have that they don't see. I figured out the difference and how to convey it to humans. We are different and we have to figure out how to say things to you humans."

Sydney was astonished by this message, and the words seemed so familiar to her. She knew that the words reflected what she had done. She felt it was coming from her own spirit. You see, she had figured out the difference between humans and the advanced peoples. It was one of the missions given to her so that the Orions could get through to humans better.

This communication was different from the prior messages she received. The ones when she was young popped into her head like it was a thought, only it wasn't. The one that came later as an adult when she was stressed was a voice, and with this communication, she felt that immense pressure where a complete message was being pushed into her brain. It was given all at one time. It was like someone gave you a paragraph to read, only you comprehended it in its entirety, in an instant.

There was another instance when she received a message where she heard a very faint voice. When she hears a voice, she cannot tell if it is male or female.

There was a day she received a vision in her mind's eye, it was a picture of Jesus' Tomb. Much of the communication her mother received was through pictures. They flashed pictures in her mind or flashed a word, and she was to interpret what they were trying to tell her. Sydney didn't think her mother always interpreted the messages correctly, so she often helped her mother to decode the channelings.

Sydney also received communication from her spirit guides. During her time of awakening, she did some guided meditations. The first time she was led to a forest and was told to imagine she was walking on a trail, and at the end of it would be one of her guides. She saw a man with lighter hair, and dirty blonde, and he was wearing an outfit from the dark ages. It had puffy red sleeves. She was thinking about what he was wearing when suddenly his clothes changed to a business suit and shiny shoes, with his hair slicked back. She saw him sitting in a chair with his legs crossed and he said to her, "How's this?" Sydney was so surprised and was hoping it wasn't her imagination.

One day Sydney had been writing all day long about her experiences and documenting everything for a speech she was going to give. She spent eight hours writing at a local coffee shop. The only way she enjoyed writing was when there was some noise in the background. She finished writing, packed up her computer, and drove home. While walking in front of the garage, she looked to her left. She did this all the time, but she didn't understand why she always looked to her left. This time she understood why. This is when she receives something. As soon as she looked left at the top of the garage, there was a large thumb in her mind's eye. It was in the "thumbs up" position, like someone was telling her, "Good job". This all happened in the few seconds she was walking to her front door. She tried to look around the thumb to see who it was, and when she finally did, she saw the same guide she saw before, her Master Guide. He was telling her "Thumbs up" for completing the speech because this is what they wanted her to do. To get the word out. To tell her story about this contact and to warn people of the environmental crisis. She was so surprised, just blown away by everything she was experiencing and seeing. She immediately called her mother and told her about the sign.

Once again, one morning Sydney woke up to a message in her mind. She had to hurry up and write it down so she wouldn't forget it. It came through like a thought, no voice. She was in awe of these messages.

That message was, *"The theory of Evolution has many missing links. The theory of Creation has no missing links."*

CHAPTER 11

Ancient Aliens

Sydney wanted to find out more about the Bible stories and about ancient structures. Her mother was getting older and sought answers to how things really happened, and to confirm if what we know is true. Sydney sat down with her mother to ask more questions to the Orions to get more clarity.

"Is it true that Moses received the Ten Commandments from God through a burning bush?"

"Yes, but the burning bush didn't mean a bush is burning. Everything you read is an assimilation of how it kind of was."

Sydney was to later assume the burning bush was an orb.

"Does the Garden of Eden exist and where is it?"

"In your mind and in your heart. The Garden of Eden is God."

"So, there's not a physical Garden of Eden?"

"There is, it's all the good things he gave you."

They told Sydney that Adam and Eve were placed near Sarnia, Canada, and this is where you want to go when bad things start to happen. It was unclear why, perhaps due to the freshwater sources.

"Did God inscribe stone tablets with the Ten Commandments then give them to Moses?"

"Yes."

"Where are the stone tablets now?"

"Still on Mount Sinai. It was taken down and was put back up at one time but is now hidden. We believe it's hidden in the mountain."

"Do some people know that it's there?"

"Yes, but not everybody."

"What was the purpose of the great flood?"

"To purify and cleanse the earth and people. A new beginning."

"Were Noah and the ark's passengers the only ones who lived through the flood?"

"No."

"Is Noah's Ark around somewhere?"

"Underwater."

"No location of where underwater?"

"The mast is in the Bering Sea."

"Were there more arks than Noah's?"

"Yes, but they weren't built like Noah's Ark. His ark was built where if it flipped over, it could ride itself."

"Did the other arks carry animals?"

"They carried vegetation."

"If Noah's Ark is in the Bering Sea, then where did Noah land and settle?"

"The ark is near Alaska. Noah went back to Jerusalem. People don't think like where is Noah's body? Where is he buried? Who was the person who wrote about Noah's Ark? If Noah was the only person left alive on the planet, how did his story survive?

How is it possible that Noah's Ark carried two of every type of animal that you see on the planet today? People need to stop and think. It's because we have been putting new animals and bugs and things on the planet."

"How did he get back there?"

"Divine powers. It couldn't have been done otherwise. It didn't go down like it's written."

"Did God part the Red Sea for Moses?"

"Not in the way it was written."

"In what way then?"

"We could tell you, but it's hard for us to describe the details of how it came about. As we go along, we will try."

The Orions described that the parting of the Red Sea was due to something similar to a tornado.

"We put so many people there on Earth and that's why you have so many different languages, different colors, everything. Not because of Adam and Eve but you still have some of our genes in you which are slowly fading away. We're worried about that because we gave you intelligence and parts of us, and you're having so many children that you shouldn't be having. You are really polluting the Earth by having too many children. Some people should have one child and others should have three and no more."

The Orions went on with more information about history:

"The Mayans disappeared because the Aztecs were eating them. They were very barbaric; the children were the most desired."

"What is the purpose of the pyramids?"

"An expression and respect. They highly respected their leaders. They considered them Gods and felt that if they didn't build them a beautiful castle for the afterlife, something bad would happen to them."

"Some people think there are records in the left paw of the Egyptian sphinx, is that true?"

"There are messages all throughout the sphinx, but they're messages people are not supposed to bother. The messages are in there for the Gods. The pyramids were built and they were never supposed to be entered once the door closed."

"Are the messages still there?"

"Yes, they are there on walls and tablets. You totally disrespect when you enter the sphinx or pyramids. It's only for the Gods and it's sacred. Very sacred."

"Are there any Bibles or other books that depict the true teachings of Jesus?"

"Was and is lost."

"Where is the lost city of Atlantis?"

"Under the Mediterranean Sea."

"Where is the Holy Grail?"

"Not to be found. It was made of wood, and it was the same as the rest of the cups they used and there was no way to tell which one Jesus used. It was just another cup that was taken from a cupboard."

"Who formed the rocks at Stonehenge?"

Beverly paused, "It starts with a C, Cohorts."

"Meaning? Like their other friends?"

"See, they don't know all the words," said Beverly.

"Did people from other planets help with that?"

"Yes."

"Who were they?"

"They built that to prove a point. It points to something."

"Do the three Egyptian pyramids line up with the Orion Constellation?"

"Yes, they do. They not only line up to that but there are also specific reasons why they were built, the way they were built, in the position they were built and down the line, it's going to show you something."

"They don't know how all of this is going to help you, but they let you know that things are progressing," said Beverly.

"With what? In all the things they've talked about?"

"The pyramids."

"The Egyptian people lost a lot when their leader died, the name starts with a T and that's when people from other planets didn't come down for a long time."

Beverly chimed in, "I think they are talking about King Tut."

"How did King Tut die?"

"Poison from a cobra. It was intentional. Nobody really knew how he was. That he wasn't all everybody thought he was. They killed him because he was going to do something really bad. He always had a lot of people killed because a lot of people were trying to kill him. You couldn't go against him at all. It was his own that killed him."

"Did Akhenaten and his family come from Orion?"

"Yes, they were the Anunnaki."

"What is the purpose of crop circles and are they made by orbs or people from other planets?"

"Some were, some weren't. The reason they were done, they're trying to show people we're here, we're playful, but there isn't anything that we found that we can't do."

"Are they made by orbs?"

"We have different spaceships that can do different things. We play too."

"By looking at a crop circle can you get energy or something from it?"

"We just wanted to let you know we're here and we're playful."

"What are black holes and do they go all the way through?"

"It doesn't go all the way through. It's like a cloud with a hole in it and it's not a nice thing to be in. It's like a garbage disposal; it sucks in trash and burns it up. Whatever goes in there burns up. The black holes are caused by gasses that burn up, and it burns a hole, from trash and cars and stuff that gets into the air. These gasses are normal and you may add to it, but it will fix itself and right now it's doing its job. Everything heals itself after a while. When the nuclear particles went into your atmosphere from the accidents, it escaped and went into the black holes. There is a lot of electricity where the stars are."

"You said sometimes fires are good for the Earth, why?"

"When you have fires on the Earth, the charcoal and ashes improve the earth; it helps the deer too. The animals roll in it to get rid of their ticks and it contains nutrients for the Earth. The Earth takes care of itself and the reason it cracks is because it has to. Think of Earth as your lung and look what happens when your lungs get plugged up. The Earth opens up in different places if the inner part gets too hot. It has to crack somewhere so it can breathe, otherwise, it would explode."

Sydney was in awe of the communication with these people and was blown away by it every time. The Orions were always there 24/7 to answered for her all the time. They would also comment on things she and her mother were doing at the time because they could physically see through their eyes. One time they were driving for a couple of hours somewhere, they commented on things they were seeing along the drive. For them to see through their eyes, they had to get their permission. It must have been through their higher selves, or their spirit at some point. That is also how they know what is going on here.

There were all kinds of things they helped with. Sydney showed her mother a document that had never been translated. Immediately, the Orions told them they needed to put the document in a mirror because it was backward, then they translated some of the words and commented that it contained many different languages.

One night Sydney was watching Ancient Aliens with her mother, and she knew there were going to be a lot of comments made, so she was ready with her recorder and notebook. The show was on Tesla, Einstein, and other geniuses.

On cue, the Orions began commenting saying they gave Einstein and Tesla a lot of knowledge but in return, they had to gather knowledge from them. This way in return it gives the Orions more knowledge of things they need to know. They said that's how they gather their information since they can't do it all themselves. When the geniuses die, the Orions collect their DNA and their brain and then inject their DNA and reform their body. The geniuses pretty much know what is going to happen to them when they die. They get a lighter body and then they become part of the group that channels people on Earth and other planets.

They said there were people like humans on Mars. They picked up people from Mars and took them to other planets because there weren't many left after a lot died due to meteors. They knew ahead of time that it was going to happen, and got a lot of the people out before it started, but they couldn't get all of them. Mars used to have nice mountains, everything flattened out due to the meteors. There weren't a lot of people on Mars like there is on Earth.

The Orions said Peru, Tibet, Egypt, and parts of South America are close to them, and they have a lot of buried tools in Peru. Those places were special places for the advanced races to meet. They built Puma Punku and explained that water runs underneath it and has a filtration system they had built.

The questioning from Sydney continued, "You said something about each planet being different?"

"There are planets out there that only have one race of peoples on it. So there is a planet with only Chinese people, a planet with only Irish people, and so on."

"What is the mystery of the Bermuda Triangle?"

"A vortex builds up in there. It's like a huge tornado that starts way up in the heavens and ends up at the bottom of the ocean and it spins like a tornado. But it doesn't happen all of the time. We saved some people from it. It is very unpredictable. It's unstable air that comes from the heavens, from way above. It's like a spinning arrow shooting out of the clouds. It causes suction."

"So, the people that don't make it, where do they go?"

"They disintegrate."

Then the Orions went on with other important information, "Earth is a fairly new planet, but we have other planets where we're trying to keep civilization going so that once Earth burns out, there will be another planet to go to, where there will be life. Some people from other planets had to leave because it was disintegrating because of all of the pollution and the water was so bad that they couldn't keep up with the filtration of the water. They had to build spaceships, like rockets, to get out of there. They had to look for another planet to go to and start all over. A lot of the ships that went first had a lot of supplies. They had only two or three people to man it, then the rest was supplies. They had to go to a planet and go underground.

It's better that when people get the knowledge to go from planet to planet, they don't get friendly and think that it's going to be a trip to Hawaii because it's just not feasible. It's just like a giraffe and a gorilla. There are planets where people live underground. They have to. They have underground streams. There's a lot of melted rock underneath and it protects the people. They live inside of the Earth. They are cave dwellers as we call them."

"Can you tell us about time travel?"

"It's hard for a normal person to understand the relativity of how you can travel to space and be there in six months, but you've lost one year of your life. As far as time travel, it is not possible to travel to the past or future of a planet."

"Are there dinosaurs on other planets?"

"Probably. All kinds of animals, a lot of strange animals. A lot of planets have no peoples, but only animals."

"Is our universe inside a bigger universe?"

"Yes, indescribable, infinity, infinity, and on and on, never-ending. When you are looking up, there are others looking down at you and others looking up at you."

"Do others travel from those other universes to this one?"

"They don't get that close. They get as close to where they can see. They don't trust you."

"Is there only one center of creation for it all?"

"No."

"Do you have counterparts in these other universes that create?"

"Yes."

"Do the humans on other planets know of us here on Earth?"

"Yes and no. They're not as advanced as you are, but they know in their minds that there has got to be more."

"If we're here, they're there. While you're looking down, others are looking up at you."

"If a person dies, does the soul sometimes go to another dimension?"

"You can't see a soul. You have to have a soul to be a spirit."

"Can DNA be changed by sound?"

"No. The only thing that can hurt DNA is if you boil the body or burn it."

"Some people think some of our vaccines change our DNA."

"It might put a bruise on it."

"The body is an intricate source, it's made up of so many channels and cells and things like that, it's unimaginable. If you cut the body up and sliced it up to put on a microscope, you would be amazed. You would have to look at it in different ways, angles, the way it's made, the way it works. Everything has a reason for being where it's at and how it works."

"I want to know if you made every race of human or did some other advanced people step in to make other races."

"We made every race of human and when two races interbreed, as an example, we can take a German and Irish person and separate and extract the Irish gene if we wanted. It's a minuscule process."

"I think they're trying to say an intricate or microscopic process because they don't know all the words," Beverly commented.

"Did we have two moons at one time?"

"If you want to call it a moon."

"What happened to it?"

"It burned out."

"Where is that moon?"

"It's in a new atmosphere. Something broke away and went into another atmosphere."

"I read somewhere there was a war and the moon was destroyed."

"It orbited out of your atmosphere into another one. It was caused by a shift in the atmosphere. It could have been from a war. There are a lot of things that happened, and we can't be everywhere all of the time. We don't know about all of them. You can't know about all of the planets there are so many of them. People thought Buck Rogers was so way out, but he was right on the money. He had visions."

"Can you tell us about our moon?"

"Your moon is an almost-burned-out planet. It used to be a sun. We have two moons, a small one and a larger one. Your moon is our small moon. A lot of your scientists don't stop and think either, but they are brilliant. They find a planet and they think there is someone on it, but you have to have a sun and a moon and it's to orbit around that planet. It has to have a gravity pull or people would have to live in a bubble or wear real heavy clothes all of the time. They would have to breathe through a tube with a helmet on, and worry about the atmosphere."

"Everything in our history we believe resides in some kind of akashic records."

"We can't know everything. It's impossible."

"What is dark matter?"

"Evil. It's something very deep, dark, dangerous, and evil."

"Where is it?"

"Everywhere. It's scary, it's the unknown, deep dark places."

"Why do we have to have something so bad?"

"So that you'll know good, better. You will be happier with good. It will make good feel better. The unknown is always dark. It's mysterious, the unknown. Scary to most people. It's in your mind."

"Are we talking about the same thing that our astrophysicists refer to as dark matter?"

"Yes and no. It's things you can't understand, scary and dark."

"Did Einstein have the last word on gravity?"

"No."

"What is the God Equation?"

"The equation does exist, but you will never get to it. It is never-ending. It never completely completes because it changes, everything changes. There is an answer but there is no answer and you'll never find it. It's like a deep hole that has no bottom. It's lined with all kinds of information about everything, but you never get to the end."

"Can you tell us a Bible story that we don't know about?"

"Most of the stories from religion were altered stories at the time to make people feel at ease. They never really told the real story the right way because at the time people couldn't handle it. They always wanted to smooth things over."

Sydney then asked them about the Phoenix Lights that happened in 1997 where people saw a very large triangle UFO flying very low. They told her that they were scanning the Earth for fractures and this way they can predict earthquakes. They said the UFO was x-raying or using sonar to accomplish this, and while they were using it, they had to get down low. When using the sonar, they cannot put up their shield, so people saw them. They had to risk being seen to accomplish the task, and this is one of the ways the advanced races are watching over us.

Sydney also asked the Orions if they would provide some kind of scientific symbol or something. They didn't say anything, so she showed her mother a crop circle and then asked them about it. The Orions replied that they needed to print it to one and a half feet in size and hold it up to the stars to find that system of stars. Then they gave her mother this, "Pi CCR q." Sydney asked what that was and they said it was the coordinates to that star system. They came around to give her what she initially asked for. Again, Sydney was floored by this information.

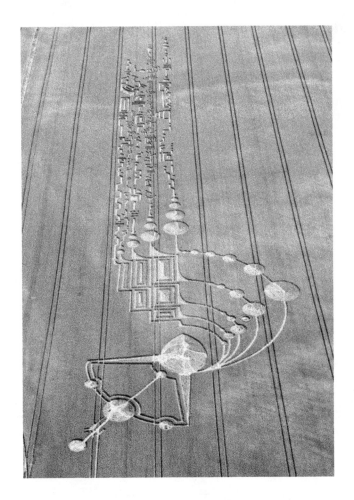

Sydney would continue to learn all kinds of things from the Orions over the next couple of years. She would get readings on people and even try to find people that were missing. Her mother didn't always get everything right because she had to try and interpret what they were telling and showing her. However, she did get a lot of very interesting information and great readings which made a lot of sense and came true.

CHAPTER 12

The One

"*Jesus' name was Jehovah in Hebrew; in every language it was different. That is what he went by.*"

Sydney was staying at her mother's house and had just gotten out of the shower when her mother came into the room. She said, "Sydney, they were telling me something this morning and they said to tell you '*Holy Mary Mother of God*' and they said they want you to think about that." It always astonished Sydney when they would address her personally. It's almost like her mother's gift was the conduit for the messages to Sydney. They said earlier that Jesus and God are one in the same. She wasn't sure what this latest message meant. So, God gave her Jesus. He gave her a piece of him. Jesus is God, and Mary is the Mother of God. Beverly continued channeling the Orions,

"*Think about it if Jesus was born of a virgin how could he be conceived or born of her vagina? That would make her no longer a virgin. So, when God says it is, it is. It would just be that it would not be born of her personal parts. Think about it. People don't think. If she had a child then she wouldn't be a virgin anymore even though the child was conceived."*

That really hit Sydney like a ton of bricks. She had never thought of that before. It made complete sense.

Beverly said, "They're trying to give me examples of what the Bible tells you."

The Orions continued, "No one asks how come, why, or how can that be? God can say it is, but he would not let Mary have a child through her body that way. She was a virgin and she and Joseph had not consummated their marriage. She did not have Jesus as a normal woman would. As a child, a brand-new child, but he was not conceived that way. She just carried him and then it was. He was not born vaginally. When God says it is, it is. In other words, he took the baby out. And that's why people do not read between the lines, they do not hear what they read."

"Mary was married to Joseph when she became pregnant with Jesus. It was an immaculate conception. God came to her and asked her to carry his child and Joseph also agreed because this would be our savior and that he was going to save the world, especially at the time of the Babylonians. God said that he was to be born of a pious woman, a very pious woman and he said it was to be and it was. She believed in good, she was pure in thought, mind, and body. Joseph was also a pious man."

"Did Mary have any other children?"

"No. Jesus was God's only begotten son. Jesus gave himself to the people and he did not take a wife. He never had children. Mary and Joseph remained virgins for the rest of their lives."

"What's God's birthdate?"

"It's not the one that you have down. Jesus and God are one in the same because he is a product of God. He was his son because he created him as a son. He put him down on Earth hoping that the people would listen to his words which they did not want to hear. They did not want to believe and then he was tortured. Then they could see what a strong person he was and that he was going to be strong to uphold fears and knowing what he knew and spreading the blessed word. He was trying to save people because he knew what his father was going to do. He sent his son to save us, to spread his word and nobody had ears or eyes because they were frightened or didn't care. And too many things overwhelmed the people. They were more afraid of dictatorship than they were of the love of Jesus in his suffering and in his words." Touched by these words, Sydney and Beverly looked at each other.

"Did Jesus have a last supper as they say?"

"Yes, he did. He really didn't know what his father had planned for him; he knew that by his death it would help get the word out. As kind and gentle as he was by his martyrism people would more or less stop and listen and know that he gave his only son. And there must have been truth in what he was saying. If everything you knew was a lie that God did not create the Earth, you're praying to nothing, then there is no hope. The last words people say are '*God please help me.*' Everybody prays to God. If there is no God, there is no devil. The devil is the bad things in life that you accept when you shouldn't. What did the Indians pray to when they needed water?"

"Was Jesus born on April 17?"

"He wasn't born December 25."

"Was Jesus' astrology sign Aries the Ram? They then showed a bull in her mother's mind, confirming Taurus."

"Where is Jesus' body?"

"He's in God's heart."

"Where's he buried?"

"His soul was left and that's in God's heart."

"What happened to his body when he died? Where was his body buried?"

"By Mount Sinai."

Then they flashed her mother a picture of a big rock with a hole in it.

"He is under the rock."

"Does anybody know about this?"

"Not anymore. You couldn't get to it anyway because of the movement of the Earth. We don't want anyone knowing where it is anyway because it's sacred."

"Do people on other planets know of Jesus?"

"Yes."

"Was Jesus born in a stable?"

"Yes."

"Was Jesus born in the Spring?"

"The day he was born it was really very nice weather. It was a perfect day, not cold, not hot. The sky was clear."

"Was he born in Bethlehem?"

"Yes."

"Can you confirm that there will be a second coming of Christ?"

"Yes."

"Were there three wise men that went to see Jesus?"

"A lot of people went to see him."

"Did they follow a spaceship which has been reported as a star?"

"They had to follow the star because they didn't have any compasses, they didn't understand all of that stuff."

"Is the Shroud of Turin the real cloth that covered Jesus after he died?"

"Yes. Very few people know where it is."

"Was Jesus' body remade so he could return and walk the Earth?"

"He arose at Easter. No, the definitive word is manifest."

"How did he manifest a body to come back?"

"It wasn't a solid body. It was a spiritual body."

"Was it a spongy body where you could touch and feel him?"

"If you did you would feel a warmth, a glow but you would not feel a solid body."

"What are the teachings of Jesus?"

"To honor his father, the Ten Commandments and what goes along with it. He taught about not stealing how bad it is, how it hurts people. To kill is wrong, and don't kill one's spirit; it means more than just the ten things. Don't steal also means don't steal somebody's pride, emotions, or feelings."

"What did Jesus eat at his last supper?"

"Breads and wines; he didn't eat meat. They had cheese and fruit. He liked nuts."

"Did Jesus do anything for entertainment?"

"He visited people and tried to comfort them."

"Who attended the last supper?"

"His followers, his bishops."

"Did Jesus have a partner?"

"No."

"Was he a virgin?"

"Yes."

"Was it Pontius Pilate who had Jesus crucified?"

"No."

"Did he let the people decide Jesus' fate?"

"They did whatever he (Pontius Pilate) wanted them to do."

"Who took his body to his final resting place near Mount Sinai?"

"His followers. The lovers of Christ."

"How old was he when he died?"

"If you want to go by that age, by how you go by years, he was in his thirties when he died."

"We are Christians. Christianity is not a religion, it's a being. Your body is a temple. A lot of the other religions are about money, power and mind control. People need to be mindful of what they choose to believe in."

"God only asks you to do ten things and one on the side; to abide by the Ten Commandments and to please go to church on his birthday."

The Orions continued, "There are a lot of naysayers in this world. As long as you know what you know, you will figure it out, but the Bible is not written the way it went down. There is a news guy who wrote a book about Jesus and that book is as close as you're going to get to the true story. It's about 85% correct."

Beverly stated, "It's the book by Bill O'Reilly, *Killing Jesus.* They said they believe he got his information also from a channeler."

Sydney decided that since the Orions do not understand our calendars, she would wait until April to begin asking them daily when Jesus' birthday was. They had said or shown her mother a bull, indicating he was a Taurus. Finally, on April 20th she asked the question again, "Is today Jesus' birthday?" They finally responded with the date of his birth which was just a few days away.

"When you are reborn you get a different birthday. We always celebrate his rebirth birthday. His birthday is the 26th of April. His first birthday was December 25th according to all the figures and different calculations and things just spinning around."

Sydney was excited about this new information and got an answer that she didn't expect. She thought that when they told her the date we have down is incorrect, she thought they meant his original birthdate. April 26th was not his original birthdate, but the date when he arose and that's what date he goes by. With this information, Sydney did what God has asked us to do. She went to a church on April 26th and gave her thanks to him, wished him a happy birthday, and expressed her sorrow for the pain he went through in death.

She did a lot of thinking about Jesus coming to planet Earth and wondered if he went to other planets as well. The Orions said he did not. He only came to the Earth. However, people on other planets do know of Jesus, but they don't know about Jesus' birth on planet Earth and his mission here. This perplexed Sydney because she wondered why Earth was special enough to have Jesus come here. Something wasn't making sense to her, there must have been an important reason Jesus was sent to Earth and no other planets. Certainly, there was evil on other planets. The Orions said it stemmed from all the different races on the planet Earth. There are other planets with races mixed in as well, but there is no planet out there like Earth. It was an experiment by the Orions to put all races that exist on planet Earth. The different races of people were clashing, and it still happens to this day. There is too much hate just because a person is different and there was always a lot of evil going on. Jesus was sent to show the way of love and caring, forgiveness, and teaching them to live and just be good people.

They said that Earth is getting to the point where no one can be trusted. The good is diminishing from people and a lot of people are on the take.

"All God ever wanted was for you to be good. He just wants you to be good."

CHAPTER 13

The Afterlife

There were so many questions running through Sydney's head that she wanted to ask. She wanted to know what happens when you die, if what we know is correct. She also wanted to know about what happens to bad people, that there should be punishment for them, other than just "not asking them to come back" as they had stated before.

"Will you please tell us about what happens when you die?" Sydney asked.

"There is a place you will go to, and we use the Pearly Gates as a for-instance because that's where you get stopped and where Saint Peter will be waiting for you. God gave you free will but in giving you free will, you create your own hell. People think there is an actual place called Hell. As far as we know, when you get to the Pearly Gates your whole life flashes before you within thirty seconds, and when it does, all that pain shoots through your body showing all of the bad things you did. And what's so bad is it hurts in your head and in your heart. It tears it out."

"When people die, are they supposed to go to the white light?"

"Everybody has to go through that. At the end of the tunnel is a force."

"Is there really a pearly gate?"

"It's like a presence of something like a gate, but it's a force field. That's where you meet your maker. You will be answering for all your bad deeds. They won't speak to you; it will be in your head. You will be answering yes and no questions more or less. But there will only be three. They will ask things like if you repent and if you are sorry and things like that."

"Do you meet God or Saint Peter or both?"

"Saint Peter will be standing by the right of God. All he does is stand there, and in your mind, he will flash the bad things. Because he gave you free will and what you did with the free will causes your hell. Bad people teach good people things, through seeing and hearing. You know you have sinned, are you sorry for all of the bad deeds you've done and you really mean it. He is very forgiving. It will be God and all of his followers and Moses."

"Why are some people saved and not others?"

"That's going to be hard to explain. People learn lessons through death that they need to learn and they need to feel because something good will come out of it. And they were old souls that needed a rest even if they were a baby. You would know if you had an old soul. People know, they just know. If humans don't think, they will never learn life's lessons. They try to be good and honest, and it comes out of their heart and soul only when they're dying."

"Is there really a heaven then?"

"Those who died, their heaven is that they get to live again for another chance at life. Heaven is a long way away. You have to go through a lot of people (incarnations) because you don't get it right. The meaning of life is to live your life. A lot of people have sinned because they didn't get to do the things they wanted to do and they missed out on life. You will never feel fulfilled. You will never rest if you don't live your life. You don't take care of yourselves; you let yourselves die too young. Your priorities are put in the wrong place. Words that you speak have no meaning without action."

"When you get it right you can go to heaven?"

"Yes, but it's almost an impossibility to be God's right hand. When you die, you just go to another planet, that's why there are so many planets because they fill up with people. You will remember bits of pieces of your previous life, but you won't understand it. That's how we get all these planets filled."

"How many souls are in heaven now?"

"Ha! Believe it or not, a lot!"

"Can God be harsh sometimes?"

"Strict. God doesn't kill people. Once they die, he takes them."

"Is it a sin to commit suicide?"

"We will be there to pick you up."

"Sydney, didn't you read up about the fallen angels?" The Orions asked.

"Yes, they came here and mated with the woman here."

"You know God put a lot of people in a lot of places, but the first people he put on the Earth didn't do well. They didn't do anything he asked. There was only one thing he asked of them that they didn't do. They didn't think they had anyone to answer to once they were put in this place. What you don't see, you ignore. That's the problem with people today."

"Why did he ask Adam and Eve to not mate?"

"Because he wanted to be the one who constructed. He took the rib from Adam and made Eve. He didn't want them to make children. He wanted to make the children and it was not the time and they broke that and it was a sacred oath. He made her from his rib, that's how he made a woman as a companion. He asked them not to do that, it wasn't time and this is why women have pain with childbirth, because of the sins of the first people."

"So, God said to go out and create and bring all things back to me."

"When he said to create, he said beauty. Your soul never dies. That's something God created. Your body dies, but not your soul."

"Where in the body does the soul live?

"Your soul lives in your brain and in your heart. When there is a heart transplant, the soul remains the same soul and there is always only one soul."

"Is there a devil?"

"There is no devil as far as what you mean by a devil. We call bad things the devil and you have to have bad things, so you can appreciate the good. People can be devils because of the mean and bad things they do. That's what you're frightened of because they have the meanness in them."

"What about spirits hanging around?"

"A lot of those people are your family who is there guiding you. And some of those people never moved on and went to the light."

"One of my friends told me there was an old lady who fostered dozens of children and she tortured them and killed them. Her mean spirit has been seen where he works."

"You need to get her to go to the light. She is still looking for the children. Tell her the children are through the light.

When spirits have not gone through the light, they still feel the pain of seeing their loved ones hurt. Once they go through the light, the hurt is lifted. Their feelings are numbed, so they can move on to guide you instead of being upset when they see something bad happen to you. You must tell them it is okay for them to move on and go to the light. Send them off with love.

A lot of times, your loved ones will wait to be reincarnated. They wait until you pass on so that they can come back next time with you as a family again."

"Angels don't have wings like you think they do."

If you remember the Islamic Terrorist named Mohammed Emwazi otherwise known as "Jihadi John" then you may remember he was the one who appeared in videos showing him cutting off innocent people's heads. After he died in 2015, the Orions told Sydney what happened to him in the afterlife. The Orions do the job for God and there is karma to pay for your bad deeds. The Orions said, "We knew he was going to be killed. We had someone present at the moment of his death who, seconds prior, had taken some of his DNA." Somehow, they can appear instantly. "We took his DNA and made him a new physical body and immediately placed him on another planet, a cold planet with nothing but wild animals on it. We allowed him to remember his life on Earth and the bad he did. He has to fight the cold and wild animals and find food every day." This was his punishment as carried out by The Orions.

Sydney remembered when she had attended a local UFO meeting and met two nice men with some extraordinary stories. One of them told a story of when he was young and fell into a river. He was caught underwater and could not free himself. He explained how all of a sudden someone reached down and grabbed him, pulling him up out of the water. He said it was a man who was tall and had on clothes that were perfect. Like they were just purchased, with creases. He wore jeans, boots, and a flannel shirt. The man told him, "Son, you should take better care in life." Just then, his brother yelled at him from down the river and asked him where he was. He said he got caught under the water and that guy picked him up. "Didn't you see him?" As he looked back and noticed the man was gone. "No, I was looking that way the entire time," his brother said. The man was saved by his Guardian Angel.

The next guy told a story of loading things into a truck at a warehouse. He was the only one at the warehouse when he heard a voice that said, "We are going to take your Uncle Robert." He turned around quickly to see where the voice came from. He was the only one there. He continued packing and then left. He drove home and saw his Uncle Robert along the way from his passing car, as Robert was homeless. He went home and finally went to bed, when at 1 am his mother came into the room. He sat straight up in bed and said, "Is Uncle Robert dead?" His mother said, "Yes, how do you know?" She explained Robert was hit by a woman in a car.

Sydney went to visit her mom again and told her these stories. The Orions responded and what they said was another "whoa" moment for Sydney.

"Sometimes we take people who are having a hard time in life or we need them for something, but we don't want people to think we are bad."

Sydney was under the impression that those voices, who whispered in his ear, directed the woman's car to hit Uncle Robert. Sydney believes this is what is meant when people say God has a plan for someone that dies too soon. The people say it's God, but they don't realize that it is advanced people doing this. The people working for God.

CHAPTER 14

The Infinite One

Sydney finally got onto a subject that she really wanted to know about, God himself. Sydney felt the Orions won't comment or provide detailed information on certain subjects for reasons unknown to her. But what she did receive was good information. She learned that God, who is referred to by the Orions as "The Infinite One" does have a physical body and lives on a planet with a lot of children. He has a body because the Orions told her that you cannot enjoy life without a body.

After a few years of having this contact, God started showing himself to Sydney in her mind's eye. It happened several times over about a year and he always showed himself in the same way. He would show himself from the shoulders up, looking over his right shoulder to Sydney. He gave her a look that answered her questions. He had loving eyes, dark hair, and a short, thick beard with a warm smile for her. He looked like he was thirty-five years old. She finally got to see him, and it was amazing. No one has ever seen the Infinite One. The feeling she had that God would reveal himself to her came true.

Sydney learned from the Orions that God is every race and that makes sense. He made all the different races of people from a part of him, so he must be every race.

"God is every race, so don't paint him white."

God lives on a planet with a lot of children because only the innocent goes to heaven. There are a lot of children in heaven and they are in physical form. So, when a child dies on Earth or another planet, the body is dead and there is no bringing it back. How do children go to God in a physical body then? God decides that a child's soul needs to rest, but he only chooses the innocent. What happens is he waits until the mother of the child that died becomes pregnant again. That same soul is given or directed to that mother and then the Orions take the embryo and grow the child on their planet so they can go to live with God. The mother experiences a miscarriage or sometimes doesn't even know she was ever pregnant.

The reason God has never physically shown himself is that if he did, everyone on the planet would straighten up. They would stop doing bad things and the whole point of free will is to advance yourselves as the best person you can be. It's about your conscience, what you do with it, and how you make your own heaven or hell on Earth. Unfortunately, there are so many Hitlers on Earth, and they have not learned to better themselves. That's why Jesus was sent down at a time when so much evil was happening, but nothing ever changed. It's now getting worse and they saw it coming. They saw the free world starting to fall at the time of JFK's killing and the reason Sydney would be born there.

Sydney received a lot of information that she wanted. She now had a better understanding of how the worlds work and who the people are who make them work. Getting information about God was the most important to her because he was a mystery. But there is still a bigger mystery. How did God come into being? The Orions would or could not tell her. Perhaps to understand that part would be too much for the human brain.

How can one man come into being and create everything you see? How was he created? This may be the question that she will never have answered.

CHAPTER 15

The Glorious One

Sydney had been on social media under a name having to do with Orion when she met a man with the name Nate Orion. There was a connection, so they kept in contact and talked often. She came to realize that this man was a nice, normal guy, a very good man who adopted two children with his wife. He was the most normal person you could meet who was also an experiencer, and he was drawn to Sydney and her contact with the Orions. They kept in contact and after a while, it became apparent why the two of them were supposed to meet. Nate had a message for Sydney.

It wasn't long into their exchange of experiences before Nate began receiving communication and channelings of drawings from a being named Doti. Nate had channeled other beings and Doti was new since meeting Sydney. This Doti person explained to Nate that he was an Orion grey who broke his programming. Doti came to Nate to assist Sydney. It became very apparent that

Nate's job on Earth was to come here to assist Sydney in her awakening. He was another holy person from Orion. Doti needed to tell Sydney something. He needed to nudge her to get her to remember who she was so she could do the job she came to do.

The information started out slowly. Over the next three months, Doti would give out a little information here and there about Sydney. Nate then relayed those messages, but it was Sydney who was to come to her own discovery. Their communication with each other continued via messenger, almost daily.

"I received an odd message as I was out to lunch. I was thinking about how we are destroying nature with our technology and pollution, and something told me that technology is nature. We don't know how to make the two as one and our bodies are not upgraded enough. I hope that didn't sound weird," said Nate.

"Not at all. I've had so many strange things happen. Since this awakening, I've had many negative entities come to me. Has this happened to you?" Sydney asked.

"Yes, one of them jumped inside my body and made me do strange things."

Nate continued, "I am receiving information about the environment and what you've been saying is correct. They're saying, if humans were true helpers of Earth as they were meant to be, then our Earth would grow fruits, vegetables, and herbs that cure every ailment. It's like we don't connect to the planet. If we take care of it, it will take care of us. Also how our technology is made from nature, so it's technically nature advanced. But it's not supposed to progress faster than what our physical bodies can currently handle. I don't know what it all means, but I never just get random thoughts like this. I don't mean to ramble; I'm just getting more to share. They say to think of the Bible verse about Adam, '*By the sweat of your brow, you will eat your food until you return. This Earth can provide all of your needs.*' Something seems to have been pulling me towards Orion to find the answers all of these years. I don't think finding you was an accident."

"No, it wasn't," replied Sydney.

Nate and Sydney ended their conversation, but the next morning Sydney checked her email to see that while Nate was at work, he sent Sydney another message.

"The ET contact I have was telling me something about you this morning. He said that you're currently one of the highest beings incarnated on Earth. Your energy field spans thousands of miles and receives other people's thoughts and prayers that are analyzed by advanced beings. Not only does your energy field receive, but also gives to those awakened to feel it. He said this is how things have always operated on Earth. There are few higher beings who are mediators between our world and other planets. These mediators, like Jesus, were known as Gods or Prophets.

You are a higher rank and there are twelve representatives of different groups on Earth, but none are as high as you and your mom because you are Theologians. There are starseeds on Earth from other planets including the Orion system. These starseed groups, twelve of them, each have a higher being representing them. You are not only representative of the Orion system, but also a Theologian. You both are higher than the others just for that fact. You both are Godly. Both you and your mom's mission is to warn about the environmental crisis. She's here to warn and to save Earth. You're here for that, but also to save souls. I don't know if that makes sense, I just wanted to relay to you what I was being told."

"Oh my God, I knew we were from the divine and we had to be connected to these people from Orion. I am the highest person on the planet. I don't know how to process all of this. My energy is very high. My energy has lashed out at others. I feel I can do things with my energy, but I don't know how to use it. I have used it without trying but just by thinking about something. For instance, I was receiving acupuncture and it was time to take out the needles. I couldn't wait for the needle to get out of my face on the right side of my cheek. I felt such a strong energy to the needle in my face and as soon as the acupuncturist removed the needle, she let out a yelp and told me that my energy pierced her shoulder.

Another time, my friend's daughter was in a car accident but didn't go to the hospital. She said her tailbone was hurting bad. It was a Sunday and so I told my friend, we should heal her together. As we were performing Reiki on her, I felt that I didn't need my friend to be there but I didn't say anything. I was super focused while having the strong desire to push my friend aside when suddenly, my friend fell back onto her bottom. With a surprised look on her face, she told me that my energy pushed her away. I turned my head to look back and told her, "I got this" as I continued with the healing. When I was finished, my friend's daughter said she felt so much better and when she went to the doctors the next day, she reported that she had a fractured tail bone."

"Your energy lashes out because you have the authority to judge. Your energy knows the innocent and the wicked. Not only is your energy powerful, but it's also pure. It doesn't mix well with impure or lower energies."

"Wow your contact, Doti is amazing. The Orions told my mother that we are their bishops, but at the time I didn't take it literally. We are different from the other Lightworkers in that we are Godly. They also said that once people realize what we have here, people will want to touch me. I don't understand what's going on here."

"Doti is telling me that you are very special, you are the one closest to God."

When he said this, Sydney felt that it seemed as though Nate pulled back, like he needed to catch himself before saying more. He stopped speaking immediately.

"Nate, I have had this feeling all my life that there was something more, something big."

"I get this very close connection with you and the Infinite One. Doti says you will figure it out."

"Nate what's strange is that I had the distinct feeling a couple of months ago that God would finally reveal himself and that I am involved somehow. The feeling was very strong."

The next day Sydney was driving in her car, where she did her best thinking, trying to figure out who she was. She said to herself, "Am I Eve of Adam and Eve?" As soon as that thought entered her mind, she got a very strong and resounding "No" in her mind which was immediately followed up with another thought. It came instantly, almost before she could digest the "NO" answer. There was no mistaking the next thought that came completely naturally, wherever it came from.

As the thought came in, she said it out loud, "I am the daughter."

But as soon as she said it, she knew she didn't want to be presumptive as to what it meant. But she did know what it meant. She is the daughter, the Daughter of God. You see, she had never even thought of any such possibility that there was a daughter. She was still in her car driving when it finally sank in, and she accepted who she was after a lifetime of confusion of the thoughts she was having. She immediately broke into tears that would not stop streaming down her face. She finally had her answer, but she was in shock. How can this be?

When she arrived home, she immediately got on the computer and contacted Nate.

"Nate, something came to me. *The Daughter* came to me. I am the daughter. The Daughter of God."

"Yes! I couldn't tell you. Doti would not allow me to tell you. I can't believe it came to you so quickly."

Both of them stunned, Sydney said, "What does this mean, am I really the Daughter of God?"

"Yes, but you need to know and feel that yourself."

"I do, with all of the things I have experienced, all of the thoughts, all of the odd things that have happened, but I am stunned, and I don't know how to process this. I knew I was someone, I just didn't know it was big like this. I don't know what to say. Oh my God, that's why all of this has happened. It's why the Orions came to us, why I have been the focus. That's what this is all about. I didn't understand why this contact happened and why suddenly we started having experiences and my mother's communication. They waited until we woke up on our own. It's the only way it could happen."

Sydney immediately remembered a conversation she had with her mother two years prior when she asked the Orions about her father's reincarnation. She thought he had reincarnated, and she wanted to know from the Orions who he reincarnated into as they said most always stay with the same family.

She asked the Orions, "Who is my father?"

The Orions said, "He is his Son."

"He is his son?" Sydney replied.

And right after that, Sydney's mother stopped the communication and said she was tired and had some things to do, leaving Sydney sitting on the couch with a confused look on her face. Sydney was confused because it made no sense as someone couldn't be reincarnated as their own child. But now this made perfect sense to her, but she was in complete shock. Her Father is his Son. In this statement, they acknowledged that God is her Father. And through what we've been told is that God and Jesus are one in the same.

"Nate, no one will ever believe this, I can't tell anyone."

"I believe you because it came straight to me as well."

The thoughts were rushing in. "When I was young, there were a couple of older ladies who told me I was going to do something very important one day. I had no idea why they would say that."

"I'm sure at the time you had no idea you were High Priestess of Orion sent to help our planet in the middle of an environmental crisis. It came to me that the Bible says Jesus was a High Priest and you're a High Priestess which means you are Godly and the way people wanted to touch Jesus for healing, they'll want to touch you. Wow! I could sense that you were more than just a bishop. I could sense you and your mom were Godly, just like the Orions said. Sydney, you are Jesus' Yin to come 2000 years after him in a dark world. You are to save the world. You are the High Priestess. The Daughter of God."

"But then Nate, how was I conceived here on Earth? I am not pure as I have married and had children. Jesus was a virgin, I am not."

"Sydney, one of the times that your mother was picked up, they took an egg from her and they fertilized it with God's seed as well as your Earth fathers' seed. You have the DNA of three people. Also, these were different times, and things were done differently, you're free of having to remain a virgin. You wanted to have children. You got to have children. As well, it is your father's seed that is pure. His DNA is pure in your body. You can't corrupt it. The DNA you have is so strong; it's why you've had these feelings all your life. It's what's reminding you. You do have a different name out there and it will come to you, or it already has."

"Nate, the name *Indiose* came to me last year."

"Did you notice the middle part "Dios" means God? Indiose means, *In God*. In (finite) dios (God) (on) e."

It was then that Sydney sat back in her chair dumbfounded as she had no idea that Dios meant "God" in Spanish. Her entire name meant the *Infinite One*. All of the puzzle pieces were coming together of her being the Daughter of God. It was all sinking in more and more. It was just so unbelievable. All of those things that happened now made sense.

Sydney didn't know how to process what she had learned. She knew it was true. Regarding this discovery, the Orions had told her mother to relate to Sydney, "You were born of that. You have always known." The Orions couldn't come out and tell Sydney because it went against the rules. It went against the rules Indiose handed to them prior to her departure to Earth.

She wanted to tell people and decided to tell a couple of people she felt needed to know. She explained it in these terms; when God made up and down, he made left and right, black and white, cold and hot, and that he made everything equal. Therefore, when he made a Son, he also made a Daughter. A Yin to Jesus' Yang, the Omega to his Alpha. This too was explained this way via Doti. The part people don't know is that she was created after Jesus' time on Earth. But that time is now. Now is the time to know about Indiose and that there is a Daughter. A Daughter of God.

The communication between Nate and Sydney continued as Doti fed more information to Nate to give to Sydney. And with all of the information sharing, she wasn't sure that Doti had been given the authority to do so or if that's why he broke his programming. Doti channeled drawings showing the relationship. Doti also explained that the people on Earth got the Holy Trinity wrong. The Holy Trinity is God, Jesus, and Indiose, and the three of them share the same spirit, the Holy Spirit. It was Indiose who was the third person of the Trinity. It was already confirmed by the Orions that God is referred to as The Infinite One, but Doti went on to explain that Jesus is called *The One,* and Indiose is referred to as *The Glorious One.* Nate sent her a channeled drawing of the triangle with IO at the top, GO at the right, and TO at the left to signify each one of them. And the triangle was clouded all around it, signifying the Holy Spirit Force.

"The Holy Trinity is God, Jesus, and Indiose."

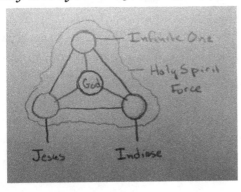

When Sydney told her mother about Doti, the Orions popped in and told her that Doti is not really his name. It's the job that he does. They said he is the "Director of Terrestrial Intelligence." When Sydney heard that, she thought to herself, "Oh my god, they are acknowledging Doti is real, and he works for the Orions. He was created by them." For Sydney, it was one connection after another telling her that this was all real. The next time she spoke to Nate and told him what Doti stood for, he was in utter shock. Nate himself had to take this all in. He was amazed and wondered how he was chosen to be the channel for the Daughter of God.

"So, me talking to you is literally like talking to one of them. Wow! You are God's right hand! Sydney, I just received this. You can transmute other people's negative energy by forgiving them. You have the power to forgive sins. Sins stay in a person's energy field until someone like you forgives them. People carry the weight of their sins. They feel guilt and shame. The negative energy makes them weak. Some do not feel comfortable confessing, but this clears it all out."

"Nate, it's coming to me that you are an assistant from Orion. You were placed here to help me awaken. You're an assistant just like my mom. Will you ask Doti how many people on Earth have telepathic communication?"

"He says it's rare, very few have true telepathic communication."

"When my mom was picked up by the spaceship in 1958, they altered her to have this telepathic communication. They said they cleared out a space in her head."

"I was visited by the greys about three times that I am aware of. One of those times it felt like they pulled me out of bed, dragged me through the walls and into a room, and sat me at a desk with a computer. There were surveillance cameras all around and I heard a voice say, "We're watching you." After that, I jerked up out of bed and my arm kept itching like they put something in there. I could still feel them in my house and was scared to get out of bed. Another time I was sleeping in my room and was awakened by one at my feet. It tried to grab me. I screamed, waking up my wife and my son and it left."

"I'm sorry they scared you. That would freak me out too," Sydney replied.

Shortly after Nate came to Sydney to assist in her awakening to who she was, he began to have some hard times personally, so the communication waned. They kept in touch here and there for the next three years, but it was time for Nate to stop all channeling and change the focus of his life. He was now getting more involved in the church. Nate fulfilled his duty to Indiose and now that work was done. His ET grey from the Orion Constellation, Doti, faded away.

Sydney was feeling not only lost but more alone than ever. Nate was gone and she had this big secret that she couldn't tell anyone. He was the only one she could talk to. It was like she was on an island all alone. She couldn't even tell her children and she couldn't talk to her mother about it who was feeling negative about God because she lost a son.

She moved on with her life, but this time she was getting her affairs in order for when she would leave this world. She had goals she had to meet with repairs to her home to leave it perfect for her children, making instructions for them, writing her will, and saving as much money as she could. She would see to it that her story was written. She was manifesting everything.

She decided to get baptized. She chose a very old mission church that was originally built for the purpose of helping poor people. That was important to her. At the baptism ceremony, Sydney felt the presence of a lot of spirits and she knew her Guardian Angel was there. Sydney asked her mother, "Mom, who is here?" "Everyone is here, but you already know that," said Beverly. All of her family that had passed on, and her Guardian Angel who usually wore a blue scarf, was wearing a white scarf for the occasion. She went on to say that the spirits formed a closed circle around them, all the family members of the people to be baptized who passed on.

Sydney went on with life as usual for the next couple of years and occasionally reflected on who she was, thinking how strange of a situation she was living. She knew not to question it because it was real. All she could do was live her best life and try to get the word out. She went on a few radio shows and wrote through social media. She wrote many letters to the President, foreign leaders, and other government representatives about pollution and how to help the homeless. She saw the world so wrapped up in evil that no one could see straight. No one could see what was happening under their very noses and even if they did, they didn't care.

CHAPTER 16

Trip to Earth

Everything was coming back to Sydney that she had forgotten in past times outside of Earth. God created Jesus and he was to be our savior, sometime after that he created Indiose. As God's right hand, she was the mediator between God and the forefathers of Orion, the Theologians of Orion. She made the decisions of how the worlds were to operate and was in charge of what information got to the people of Earth and other planets. When it came to Jesus, his job was to visit people in their dreams and comfort them.

The other planets are in different stages of their evolution. There are planets in the horse and buggy stage and others in medieval times. There are universes within universes, but the Forefathers of Orion only oversee, under Indioses' direction, the planets in this universe. The Orions work with the other advanced races to oversee the planets, to help guide them, teach them, and protect them. It's always been this way, it's just that the people of today have not realized that people such as the Egyptian leaders were from the Orion Constellation. They were the Annunaki sent from Orion to teach the people how to find water, grow food, and build.

Sydney came to planet Earth for many reasons, but she felt strongly about how it happened. Sydney or should I say, Indiose, held a meeting with the Forefathers from the Orion Constellation and informed them that she would go to Earth to see for herself the conditions there. They could see that the warnings to the people of Earth throughout the years had gone ignored and this would be the last effort to get people to change, to fix their pollution, and be better people, the way God intended. She would take an assistant, and together they would be a team to get the word out about Earth's inevitable destruction. She would choose one of their own holy people from their group and this would be the mother she would be born to on Earth.

The Infinite One himself had also informed the elders that she was to live life on Earth just as everyone else, as was done with Jesus. She was not to be assisted and she would have to live with all the ups and downs in life without help from the Orions. She would have free will and be able to live her life the way she wanted. She was to be good or bad, do wonderful things, bad things, and make mistakes. She was to learn lessons just like everyone else. She realized her lessons included experiencing what the homeless and people with illness go through. And she would be tested on knowing how to handle tough situations and doing the right thing with interpersonal relationships. Unlike Jesus, she could have children. This was a more modern time, and it would be different from when Jesus came to the Earth. Even her conception was different.

The times she had come to Earth prior were for her preparation for this final life on Earth, but in her training, she had died too young because she took herself out. This time she would have to come back and stick it out, as it was extremely important for her mission. It would become necessary that Sydney have children to keep her from returning home too soon before the job was done. She was an extreme empath and her time on Earth would be very painful due to how badly she was going to be treated.

When it came time, each one would shed their body which would be stored in capsules in underground caves, then their souls would enter their new earthly bodies. Their bodies would await their return many years later with the Orions guarding them. The assistant from Orion was born first who would be Indiose's mother and vehicle to Earth, with the gifts to help awaken and guide her. Indiose would be born twenty-three years later, and the preparation would then start. It had to be done this way for their body to acclimate to the atmosphere of Earth.

She would be born on Earth and not remember anything from her past life in the Orion Constellation. Throughout her life, she would receive telepathic messages and prodding from the Orions to help guide her and wake her up to her mission and to who she was.

It became apparent that her body did a job that she didn't realize. Her energy spanned thousands of miles and picked up people's thoughts and prayers. At an unconscious level, she was a translator and interpreter to the Orions for what was happening on Earth. They do this by reading her thoughts – the many thoughts she had throughout her life. There were so many instances over the years that she thought about how people were and dissected them and really tried to understand them. She understood that people were very complex; she saw it, but she had no idea why she was fixated on figuring out the complex human mind.

She sent herself to Earth to find out what the difference was between the advanced races and humans and why they could not understand humans. She did this so that they knew how to get through to them, how to communicate with them because all their warnings failed. The Orions created a being they didn't even understand themselves.

They are so different from humans. After all these thousands of years, she found out the difference. Some of it could be explained as humans being very fearful and not using their brains the way they should. They live in fear and take most things told to them in a negative way. They only see the negative spin and this causes many problems. This is how rumors and wars start. If there were two ways to take something, the human will most always take the negative interpretation. And when very smart humans get together in a group, they make horrible decisions. The best way to get through to people is by using the right words. The Orions told her she had a gift for the words. "The WORDS! The words are so important," they said. The remainder would only be able to be relayed via feeling. A strong feeling of how humans were and then relaying that to the Orions for them to pick up on, a feeling she couldn't explain.

She was a healer; she healed in many ways. She healed with her hands, with her words, and her forgiveness of their sin. She came to warn the people. She came to make Indiose known. She came to save the world.

Sydney was much like the people from Orion. She didn't like long names and words; she was blunt and straight to the point, with a dry sense of humor. She would remove herself from the Earth at the age of eighty-six years old. With her sense of humor, to eighty-six herself she figured would be the perfect age to take herself from this planet. She would have done all she could do for the people of Earth. She would age unlike any other time she had been to Earth prior. On her planet she never aged; she remained a stunning beauty, but she was to become an old woman for the first time, and she wasn't excited about it.

Sydney, or should I say Indiose, found that even though being on Earth had been very difficult for her, she was really going to miss it and the good people she met, as well as her family. With all of the challenges, at least she had some good times with friends and family. She enjoyed the small things, and she was proud of how creative people are and thankful for the good souls on Earth. She especially enjoyed great movies and music from different genres, but her favorite had to be sixties and seventies music.

She wants the people to know that life is short, too short for all of the evil, the fighting, and hate. It's to where no one can be trusted, not even friends. She wished for people to live a better life and enjoy it more. Money was the worst invention ever. Turn off the television and social media and go out and enjoy the simple things in life. All the evil makes life unenjoyable. The wars need to end. The people need to come together. We need to celebrate the different people on the planet, instead of hate. Earth is the only planet that has all the different races and how blessed are we that we get to experience different people, their cultures, the things they make, and the wonderful food.

She felt very strongly that at some point in the near future she would be taken aboard a ship for a meeting. She would be picked up and meet these advanced people on a ship. She would see people that she knew throughout her life, and she would be so surprised that those people were all part of this. The two older ladies would be there. In her daily life, occasionally she sees someone that she knows is "one of them." They pay particular attention to her; they stare at her and offer to help her. They know who she is.

CHAPTER 17

The End of the World

People will perish if the pollution on Earth is not turned around. It's already happening, but people are not talking about it. They are dying of cancer and people are not living as long anymore. The air, earth, ocean, and freshwater sources are all polluted. The animals eat food grown from the ground, you eat those animals and food grown from the ground. But at some point, the Earth will be so polluted that you won't be able to grow food. Then you will need to move to hydroponics, but that won't work for long either. Your water and air are polluted, and treating it with chemicals will treat the minerals right out, which are essential to your body.

It can get worse, and many will die. Women will not be able to have children any longer. The population would thin out and it would be all downhill from there. The year 2076 was given as the timeframe that the pollution needs to be turned around. It needs to start now, however, because it takes so long for the entire planet to follow suit. It takes decades to clean up the planet, move to clean energy, and stop producing harmful products. It can be done, and the people can prolong life on Earth for many hundreds, perhaps thousands of years. The Earth itself is already dying, but it will take eons before the planet is dead. But there is hope because the Orions stated that if we start now, we can avert a catastrophe.

In the Bible, you've been told that Jesus would be back. This is true, but have you ever thought of why he would come back and when? When it's nearing the end of the world is when he will come back, but Indiose will be with him. A trumpet will sound for twenty minutes, then Jesus and Indiose will appear in the sky for everyone around the planet to see all at once. People will come out of their businesses and their homes. They will awaken from their sleep and go outside. They will be given a blessing and receive a feeling of unconditional love in their body that will last for two minutes. They will be given the feeling in their mind that they are being saved and to not be afraid. By this time the people would already know about Indiose. They will look upon the people with love and then fade away.

Moments later, Orions ships will appear in the sky and those remaining lives on Earth will be taken by the Orions' greys, guided by the other advanced races, to newly prepared planets. Upon being placed on the planet, the memories of their life on Earth will be erased. They will continue on with life on another planet and the souls of their family members who passed on will be reincarnated to be with them. This way they keep the same families together. It's been this way for eons.

Word needs to get to the people. There isn't a lot of time.

CPSIA information can be obtained
at www.ICGtesting.com
Printed in the USA
BVHW041114290522
638353BV00003B/13